Do it The Lazy Way

1. Time flies when you're having fun, right? So use your favorite show to keep you entertained while you exercise, and you may not even feel like you're working!

2. Use smaller plates and bowls to automatically reduce portions. (Shrink your frosted flake habit by a cup, and you can lose six pounds a year.)

3. When home, always wear your favorite tennis shoes. Even a single flight of stairs in your own home can help you win the battle of the bulge.

4. Just say yes to sex (safe, of course)! Men, try Yohimbe, an inexpensive aphrodisiac instead of some of the more expensive products on the market!

5. If you must lie down after eating, lie on your left side. This will help keep your stomach below the esophagus, keeping acids down with the help of gravity. No heartburn!

*One luxurious
bubble bath*

*Access to most comfortable
chair and favorite TV show*

*One half-hour massage
(will need to recruit spouse, child, friend)*

*Time to recline and listen to a favorite CD
(or at least one song)*

cut

Do it

6. "Be an Optimist: When your computer crashes before a deadline, you probably feel like jumping in bed and pulling the covers over your head—but don't! Stay positive and keep perspective!

7. Lose weight while you sleep by taking a harmless pill! The pill is chromium, which burns up fat.

8. Schedule all your workouts, massages, vacations, just as you do a doctor's appointment.

9. Eat 'em up, rub 'em on, hot peppers are good for what ails you because they contain capsacin, which is a great pain reliever and destroys inflammation!

10. Eat beans. The folate from every kind of bean can battle heart disease and curtail cancer.

COUPON

COUPON

COUPON

COUPON

Stop Aging

Stop Aging

Judy Myers

The Lazy Way™

Macmillan • USA

This book is dedicated to my father, who continues to exemplify youth into his 90s. Also to my mother, who recently passed, who was a never-ending source of encouragement and inspiration. I would also like to dedicate this book to my loving children: Michael and Julietta, and my present grandchildren, Jesse David and Avriella, and future grandchildren and great grandchildren, whose legacy is clear.

Macmillan Publishing books may be purchased for business or sales promotional use. For information please write: Special Markets Department, Macmillan Publishing USA, 1633 Broadway, New York, NY 10019.

International Standard Book Number: 0-02-862793-8
Library of Congress Catalog Card Number: 98-89558

00 99   8 7 6 5 4 3 2 1

Interpretation of the printing code: the rightmost number of the first series of numbers is the year of the book's printing; the rightmost number of the second series of numbers is the number of the book's printing. For example, a printing code of 99-1 shows that the first printing occurred in 1999.

Book Design: Madhouse Studios

Page creation by Eric Brinkman, David Faust, Heather Pope

Printed in the United States of America

You Don't Have to Feel Guilty Anymore!

IT'S O.K. TO DO IT *THE LAZY WAY!*

It seems every time we turn around, we're given more responsibility, more information to absorb, more places we need to go, and more numbers, dates, and names to remember. Both our bodies and our minds are already on overload. And we know what happens next—cleaning the house, balancing the checkbook, and cooking dinner get put off until "tomorrow" and eventually fall by the wayside.

So let's be frank—we're all starting to feel a bit guilty about the dirty laundry, stacks of ATM slips, and Chinese takeout. Just thinking about tackling those terrible tasks makes you exhausted, right? If only there were an easy, effortless way to get this stuff done! (And done right!)

There is—*The Lazy Way*! By providing the pain-free way to do something—including tons of shortcuts and time-saving tips, as well as lists of all the stuff you'll ever need to get it done efficiently—*The Lazy Way* series cuts through all of the time-wasting thought processes and laborious exercises. You'll discover the secrets of those who have figured out *The Lazy Way*. You'll get things done in half the time it takes the average person—and then you will sit back and smugly consider those poor suckers who haven't discovered *The Lazy Way* yet. With *The Lazy Way,* you'll learn how to put in minimal effort and get maximum results so you can devote your attention and energy to the pleasures in life!

THE LAZY WAY PROMISE

Everyone on *The Lazy Way* staff promises that, if you adopt *The Lazy Way* philosophy, you'll never break a sweat, you'll barely lift a finger, you won't put strain on your brain, and you'll have plenty of time to put up your feet. We guarantee you will find that these activities are no longer hardships, since you're doing them *The Lazy Way*. We also firmly support taking breaks and encourage rewarding yourself (we even offer our suggestions in each book!). With *The Lazy Way*, the only thing you'll be overwhelmed by is all of your newfound free time!

THE LAZY WAY SPECIAL FEATURES

Every book in our series features the following sidebars in the margins, all designed to save you time and aggravation down the road.

- **"Quick 'n' Painless"**—shortcuts that get the job done fast.
- **"You'll Thank Yourself Later"**—advice that saves time down the road.
- **"A Complete Waste of Time"**—warnings that spare countless headaches and squandered hours.
- **"If You're So Inclined"**—optional tips for moments of inspired added effort.
- **"The Lazy Way"**—rewards to make the task more pleasurable.

If you've either decided to give up altogether or have taken a strong interest in the subject, you'll find information on hiring outside help with "How to Get Someone Else to Do It" as well as further reading recommendations in "If You Want to Learn More, Read These." In addition, there's an only-what-you-need-to-know glossary of terms and product names ("If You Don't Know What It Means/Does, Look Here") as well as "It's Time for Your Reward"—fun and relaxing ways to treat yourself for a job well done.

With *The Lazy Way* series, you'll find that getting the job done has never been so painless!

Series Editor
Amy Gordon

Managing Editor
Robert Shuman

Editorial Director
Gary Krebs

Development Editor
Alana Morgan

Director of Creative Services
Michele Laseau

Production Editor
Mark Enochs

Cover Designer
Michael Freeland

What's in This Book

The Key to Longevity—You Can Fool Mother Nature!

When I turned 59 years young this year, my friends just went nuts! They were slack-jawed when I revealed my age, especially since I had lied about it for years! It was obvious they thought my age meant I should be playing in shuffleboard tournaments in Florida. After all, I am a divorced woman, living and working in New York City, producing and hosting a weekly health and fitness television show. I compete in body-building and fitness contests against women in their late teens and 20s, and take hip-hop dance classes three times a week. I also perform on roller skates in Central Park every weekend. For some reason, these friends act like I should receive a medal of valor for being so actively involved in my grandchildren's formative years. Who knew I could do all of this at such an "advanced" age?

When I competed in the first Ms. Grandma of the Year beauty pageant and won in 1997, the audience and participants were wowed by the fact that I could do splits and one-armed push-ups on roller skates. Since then, I have appeared all over the world via websites and television talk shows to reveal my secrets for looking better and feeling younger in my 50s than I did in my 30s! I want to share with you my secrets to slowing down the aging process with tips and tricks that take very little time and energy. I will also try to prove to you that we were meant to use our bodies and minds throughout the duration of our lives, not just in our earlier years.

Keep in mind that having had over 30 years in the professional field of physical and health education has given me a "leg up" on most of my colleagues!

I currently operate a private practice at my office, The Beverly Hills Fountain of Youth Clinic, which has a satellite office in New York City. I aim to give my clients back 10 to 15 years by offering alternative medicinal applications. These techniques are all designed to help you stay lean, young, and sexy! My practice has provided a virtual laboratory for me and my theories, and it has definitely given me the knowledge and experience to pass on to you.

No other author who has written about anti-aging or longevity has the combined practical and professional knowledge that I have, or is a living testimony that their program works. When I reviewed a list of comparative books, I discovered that most of the authors have not achieved anything close to what they are writing about! Never mind the fact that none of their graduate or post-graduate work had an emphasis on any of the areas that are so important: fitness, nutrition, and health education.

Traditionally, information about the aging process was gathered from studies and case histories of relatively small groups of people, usually medical patients. Likewise, most books on longevity are written by psychiatrists, MDs, and non-professionals in the health field. Their educational scope is limited for effective application. What can be really scary is that none of the authors seem to have truly applied any semblance of what they preach to their own lives.

This easy-to-understand book will answer all your questions about reversing the aging process with tips, techniques, and suggestions, along with tons of advice such as: "Do I really need the growth hormone treatment at that spa in Mexico?" and "Do I have too much body fat?" I'll cover everything from weight loss strategies—including why conventional diets don't work and multi-cultural eating—to terrific new foods you can really enjoy and lose fat in the process. There are lists to help you find the best non-junk food snack foods and convenience foods that will help lower cholesterol and body fat. But wait, there's more! I'll also share with you the advantages of learning new skills, finding the right trainer, training smart, and recovering fast. Still want more? I'll answer such questions as: "Can biofeedback control my heart rate?" and "What is a spiritual healer?" and "Is there an anti-hot flash diet?" and "Is Viagra safe?"

What took me years to discover, you can learn in a short time—just a matter of hours—and be able to use this knowledge to short-circuit the aging process right away! The knowledge will be a plus, but the application of it will turn back the clock for you. Remember: You will never get better at tennis just by talking to the racket salesman, but you will get a sensational game together by taking lessons from the tennis pro.

What I am about to share with you is more than a theory. It is a lifestyle that can move you beyond today's stereotypical concepts of aging. This book is dedicated to making you laugh and keeping you young. I realize that some of you feel limited by the years you have left, but if you are willing to tackle your own fears about aging, exercise, nutrition, stress, medical information, and the like, you will have a right to your high expectations about the quality of life you enjoy from now on. You have to work toward this goal. By accepting personal responsibility for your lifestyle and health habits, and consequently for your own well being, you help insure that you will enjoy the best return and the highest level of satisfaction from your 40s, 50s, 60s, and on.

You will need faith in yourself, and this comes from being responsive to change and from having a sense of the future. This book says that if you are 45 to 55 years old, physically your health status could equal that of someone 25 to 34 years old. If you are a woman and maintain this lifestyle, you can add as much as seven years to your life span. If you are a man and adhere to the principles, you can add 11 to 12 years to your life. Remember: Chronological age is only a number, and you can beat the aging process—you can extend your youthful years! But really, it's never too late to get in shape physically, mentally, and spiritually.

Purchasing this book may just be the best investment you will ever make.

THANK YOU...

To my father, George C. White, who at 90 years young is the most amazing man who still has all his "marbles" and continues to "rock on" as a consultant and author in his field of engineering. He is my inspiration and confirmation that age is only a number! Also to my mother, an author of 27 published novels, who aptly called me "the oldest living teenager." She always believed I could do anything I set my mind to; nothing was too bizarre a feat. She always said, "T'aint no reason you can't."

I pass this entire legacy down to my two children, Julietta and Michael. Julietta has accomplished her dream to perform in *Cats* on Broadway, and Michael has become a jet pilot. They worked for it because I told them they could achieve what they believed.

Thank you to my two wonderful agents, Ann Elmo and Andrea Abecassis, for their belief in me, their constant support, and their professionalism in their attention to the details.

Special thanks to Amy Gordon, my editor, for sticking with me in the "tough times" and seeing this work to its finality. I could not have done this without her. Thanks to Alana Morgan who was the "cornerstone" of this project in staying on top of it on a daily basis and in constant communication to steer me to its finality.

STOP AGING The Lazy Way

Finally to those in the fitness and bodybuilding community and the print and television industry for constantly covering my outrageous athletics feats to help promote awareness and give exposure to the reality of staying youthful in the aging process. Thanks also to my skaters for giving me constant attention and support. Thanks to my children and grandchildren who call me the original "bionic woman." Thank you to God for providing me with the inspiration to write this.

Part 1

The Anti-Aging Tool Kit

Are you too lazy to read "The Anti-Aging Tool Kit?"

1 Does the mountain of cosmetics in your bathroom sometimes make you nervous? ☐ yes ☐ no

2 Does the vast array of cosmetic products out there make you consider staying at home instead of having to choose one? ☐ yes ☐ no

3 Are you convinced that plastic surgery is for Hollywood starlets only? ☐ yes ☐ no

Beauty in a Jiffy

Getting out of bed is one thing, but looking great when you leave your home is another. During the work week, I can shower, blow-dry my hair, put on my makeup, eat breakfast, and be out the door in 16 minutes. I learned these secrets way back in my days as a flight attendant. I used to dread those freezing early-morning flights out of Chicago and wanted to stay under the warm covers 'til the last moment. Then I learned that most health and beauty regimens can be accomplished in minutes, without sacrificing the results.

You can always reserve one day—say during a weekend or holiday—to get scrubbed, polished, buffed, and pampered, but right now, you want to circumvent a typical 45-minute blow-dry or laborious makeup routine. Before we move on, I want you to realistically look at your expectations of the results of the products you might have purchased. You are not going to look like Cindy Crawford or Brad Pitt. What you are doing is taking a three-pronged approach to looking and feeling better about yourself as you hear the biological clock ticking.

QUICK ☐ PAINLESS

Become wrinkle-less with this helpful hint for prevention: wear sunglasses, don't squint, and be sure to get enough sleep every night.

With my system, you are investing in yourself on every level. Stop feeling guilty for treating yourself lovingly! You will find that this self-improvement process and age-defying attitude will spill over to your physical and mental life, which I will talk about in the following chapters, but first, we have to get you back on the highway, in the express lane to beauty!

EQUIP YOURSELF!

First things first: For every job, there is the proper tool, and I have created my own anti-aging tool kit. It's a fishing box with three shelves that I bought at a flea market several years ago, and I keep it stowed away under the sink. I am constantly replenishing supplies such as powder, foundation, blushes, moisturizers, and exfoliates. Then there are all those creams, emery boards, and so forth for my hands, feet, legs, and hair. Some of the products are expensive, and some are not. Do know, however, that should the occasion arise (and it frequently does), I can be confident that "I'm ready for my close-up."

Where to Find It

I used to spend a great deal of money on expensive treatments, lotions, and creams. I soon realized I had to take more time in considering my purchases and how to stretch the almighty dollar to keep on saving. So how and where do you get more for your money? Look no further than right here!

- Department stores
- Chain stores

- Drug stores
- Salons
- Health food stores

As an Alternative

Private labels, which are sometimes manufactured at the same plants that pack the brand-name items, can cost from 20 to 50 percent less and are identical to the original. Why blow your hard-earned money? Here are some of the places you can get more bang for your buck when it comes to purchasing these kinds of supplies:

- Ray's Beauty Supply: 212-757-0175
- J.F. Lazartigue: 800-359-9345
- Adrenaline bars at health food stores
- Bio-therm: 888-BIOTHERM
- Bobbi Brown Essentials: 212-980-3232
- Dr. Scholl's: 800-766-6465
- Phyto-Pro from Phytotherathrie: 800-55-PHYTO
- Supersolano hair dryer: 800-323-3942

FOUNTAIN OF YOUTH KIT

Anyone can look younger with a pharmacy's worth of stuff in their bathrooms, but why deal with all of that stuff when there are a few simple yet essential items that can go the distance? The following list is what I consider the basic "fountain of youth kit," and I'll tell you why these items are indispensable, as well as where to find them!

YOU'LL THANK YOURSELF LATER

Decrease your salt intake to prevent fluid retention that causes puffiness under the eyes.

- Hair supplies
- High-powered blow-dryer (compact size)
- Mousse
- Frizz controller
- Rapid drying shampoo
- Johnson's Baby Shampoo

IF YOU'RE SO INCLINED

Vaseline petroleum jelly takes care of everything: it's an ointment for the lips, an eye cream, and eye makeup remover all in one.

Bargains

I've said it before, and I'll say it again: there is absolutely no need to spend exorbitant amounts of money when others are willing to give you the same thing for less! The following items are low-risk but high-yield:

- **Dax Wave and Groom $2.29.** Annihilates the frizzies when smoothed on the back and ends of your hair, and it can moonlight as a hair-texturizing lotion. Mix Dax with a gel for a styler that gives hair softness and will hold.

- **Dippity-Do Hair Gel $3.34 (8 oz. jar).** Controls hairstyles, smoothes curly hair, sleeks back, holds a part, and perfects the Jim Carrey *Pet Detective* look. It can also double as an eyebrow shaper that could withstand a hurricane. Sweep a light amount over each eye.

- **Aqua Net Professional All-Weather Spray $1.19.** Delivers maximum hair holding power, no matter what. It also doubles as an anti-static guard, killing cling. De-electrify your hairbrush by spritzing it on your brush.

You Gotta Have It

These items are absolutely and unequivocally indispensable! If you don't have them already, run, don't walk, to pick up these little items!

- Anti-aging moisturizer
- Retin-A
- Concealer
- Cream highlighter for eyes
- Black mascara
- Eyelash curler
- Sheer lipsticks
- Cosmetic brush
- Deeply tinted gloss
- Cream blush
- Translucent powder
- Anti-aging bargains

LITTLE TRICKS TO SWEAR BY!

Shh! Is anyone looking? These little tricks are secrets to hold close to your heart! From enhancement to just making your life easier, try some of these on for size!

- **Coty Airspun Powder $6.75.** Covers pores with a few blots of a fluffy powder puff. Brush on a darker shade between your breasts to give the illusion of cleavage. With a light dusting on your lips, you can make lipstick stay on for a long time.

YOU'LL THANK YOURSELF LATER

Don't leave home without one of these: a large Ziploc bag to carry your favorite supplies such as a foldable hair brush, a toothbrush, a packet of three makeup brushes, a pencil sharpener, and a miniature can of hair spray. And ladies, don't forget to include your favorite lipstick!

- **Q-tips $3.25 (125 sticks).** Performs numerous functions, from blending eye shadows to fixing home manicure mistakes. Can even function as a lip liner!

- **Maybelline Great Lash Mascara $5.00.** Get clump-free lashes at a guilt-free price—or cover up your gray hair! Take a gray strand and apply one swish of the mascara on—you're gray no more!

- **Noxzema Skin Cream $2.69.** This acts as a face wash and stimulates your face with its ingredients of menthol and eucalyptus. It's also a sure bet to use as a shaving cream because it is so creamy. You can even use it on your feet for a "foot mask."

The Not-So-Necessary-but-Still-a-Great-Idea Beauty Budget

You don't need these little guys to keep a young face, but they can be useful!

- **Max Factor Pan-Stik makeup, $7.75.** Hides undereye circles. It can also be used as a base for eye shadow and to hide redness of skin and to even out skin tone. You can even use it as a lipstick base; lips will look fuller, and lipstick will stay on longer.

- **Pond's Cold Cream $5.49 (6.1 oz. jar).** Removes makeup and moisturizes skin when you want to do both. Different flavors (such as rose) can be used as an aromatherapy treatment—a good stress-buster!

- **Revlon Super Lustrous Lipstick $7.75.** Cherries in the Snow has always been considered a classic. It is red

YOU'LL THANK YOURSELF LATER

Fast makeup application requires fewer products and a broad brush approach. This should take you no more than five minutes. Watch out! Too much makeup can highlight wrinkles.

but not too blue or orange. It complements the more mature skin.

- **Chap Stick Lip Balm $1.29.** Gotta protect those dry lips and keep them from the harmful effects of the sun, wind, cold, and snow. Plus, use it as a lipstick base. The colorless balm won't affect the shade. You can also use it before you climb into bed to soften cuticles and extra-dry patches on your nose, cheeks, and chin.

Getting Nailed—Must-Haves

Polishing up should cover everything, from the top of your head down to your toes, so don't forget about the importance of those nails! These little items will help you hit the nail on the head!

- Polish remover
- Tissue
- 100 percent cotton balls
- Nail clippers
- Emery board
- Fast-drying ridge filling base coat
- Fast-drying polish
- Lee Press On Nails
- Pumice nailbrush
- Foot pumice
- Olive oil

IF YOU'RE SO
INCLINED

When you take a nap or right before you go to bed, put cream on as a mask. Leave it on for 12 minutes, with music in the background. Then rinse it off.

THE FAST TRACK TO LOOKING AS YOUNG AS YOU FEEL!

Now that you've got the tools, you're ready to kick Father Time's butt! Just follow these directions, and you'll be on the fast and lazy track to looking as young as you feel!

The Heads Up Routine

We all want to put our best face forward, and here's the quickest way to get you there!

1. Dry wet hair by blowing it back and forth until almost dry, and then apply your mousse.

2. While waiting for the mousse to be absorbed, quickly apply moisturizer to your face.

3. Finish blow-drying your hair. Apply frizz control.

4. Apply your foundation by using a wet sponge.

5. Rub in styling cream and blow-dry your hair in big sections, starting from the crown.

6. Wrap as much hair as possible around your brush and blow-dry for 15 seconds. Slowly unravel hair so that it is smooth and falls into place. (It helps to have a great haircut.)

7. Now to finish your makeup! Eyes can be finished in seconds as long as you use quick, sweeping strokes.

8. Dab concealer on key spots with the tip of your finger.

YOU'LL THANK YOURSELF LATER

You should use light polish and sheer colors. These will show less mistakes, smudges, and scratches.

9. Use your finger to apply cream highlighter on the lid. This will give the illusion of larger eyes.

10. Apply lipstick with one full sweep.

11. Add some crème blush, rubbed in with fingers; it lasts longer than powder.

12. Finally, a few swooshes of translucent powder using your cosmetic brush, and you're done!

Give Yourself an Edge

These little tricks can't be picked up in any store, but you can incorporate them into your daily routines, and you'll wonder how you never thought of it before!

- Put out your clothes and shoes the night before to save time.

- Give yourself a facial, exfoliating, and then apply a moisturizing mask on Sunday evening of each week.

- Wash and blow-dry your hair the night before work.

- Whiten your smile with an at-home bleaching kit.

- Do the do—change your hair. Cut it, creating a more tousled look. The bubble, with every strand in place, went out with the disco era. It adds years.

Cutting It to the Quick

You've got the stuff, now for the routine! Time to buff and polish!

- **Toes and fingers.** Sure, when it comes to toes, you may be thinking "No one can see them, so why

Congratulations! Now that you have learned this lightning-fast technique, you can hit the snooze button and sleep an extra 15 minutes tomorrow.

The Lazy Way

IF YOU'RE SO
INCLINED

Spur of the moment dinner date? A compulsion to go barefoot? Okay, Don't fret! You can give yourself a great manicure or pedicure in a flash!

bother?" But looking beautiful means feeling beautiful, so do it for yourself!

1. Remove polish and cut straight across nails.

2. Use an emery board to smooth the edges of the nail.

3. Separate toes with pieces of cotton balls.

4. Put on one coat of base polish.

5. Put on one coat of regular polish.

6. After polish is dried, take a little olive oil, rubbing it on and around each toenail.

BEING PREPARED FOR AN EMERGENCY

Suppose you are having a last-minute family get-together or you have just traveled for hours, and you can't do the whole facial routine. You just want a secondhand one, something to perk you up. You don't want to take your makeup off. Is this possible to do? Sure! Here's how:

The "Be Prepared for Anything" Kit

Make sure you have the following items in your cosmetic bag (and anti-aging kit), and you'll always have what you need to "Be Prepared for Anything!" Your skin will look radiant and glowing, and you will feel like a new person.

Eye mask
Linen hand towel
Cream cleanser

Ready, Set, Go!

1 Put on eye mask to cover your eyes; but be careful, you don't want to smudge your eye makeup!

2 Massage cleanser into skin in circular motions.

3 Soak cloth in hot water, squeeze all the water out, and place on face for four seconds.

4 Repeat the heat treatment.

5 Run cold water over cloth.

6 Place on face and press.

FINE TUNING

The ageless boomers—that's you and me—are the pioneers of life's journey. We are the ones always seeking new frontiers, taking classes, and traveling the world solo, with the inherent belief that we can always improve ourselves, that there is a better way. That's why you're still reading my book.

You might be able to transform yourself into a youthful version of your old self. Maybe you will have a lover 20 years younger or drop out of your day job to pursue something more fulfilling. One thing for sure is that you will have that inner glow, strength, and beauty that will make you ageless. As Billy Crystal states in his Fernando Lamas sketch, "It's not how you feel, you schnook, it's how good you look!"

A COMPLETE WASTE OF TIME

The 3 Worst Things You Can Do for Your Face Are:

1. Facial massages—they only give your face a temporary glow.

2. Facial exercises—they can't build muscles to fill up wrinkled area.

3. Electronic facial machines—these cost almost $500, and they are only temporary skin stimulators.

Baby Those Baby Blues

As we age, our vision diminishes due to macular degeneration. Sunlight is one of the main reasons our vision becomes impaired. You must shield your eyes.

Hearing Healthier

There's a vast amount of research out there regarding how and what we hear, so take advantage of it! We now know what the danger zones are and how to prevent premature hearing loss, so think about what you subject your ears to on any given day. Some of you may wonder why you would ever need to carry around a set of earplugs, especially if you don't work in the entertainment industry. But believe it or not, there are a lot more ear-assaulting things in everyday places than you might think!

If you want to preserve your hearing, carry earplugs to ease the assault of noise levels above the ear-piercing sound (90-decibel limit)—think about it the next time you're on the subway. Research shows that almost 60 percent of health clubs play music above 110 dB and vacuum cleaners, movies, and crying babies all exceed the danger zone. When it comes to earplugs, "Use it or lose it."

Getting Time on Your Side

	The Old Way	The Lazy Way
Making up	35 minutes	3 minutes
Doing the do	45 minutes	6 minutes
Toeing the line	30 minutes	4 minutes
Using moisturizers	12 minutes	3 minutes
Reapplying makeup	16 minutes	4 minutes
Getting dressed	25 minutes	4 minutes in the morning

Mirror, Mirror on the Wall—Plum or Prune?

Mirror mirror, so big and bold—why do I feel so young and look so old?"

Does this have a familiar ring? When you look in the mirror, do you feel as if you have so many wrinkles that a Sharpei dog looks like your next-of-kin? No need to panic! Looking young and vigorous is achievable, and that tired look can disappear. This is about creating an overall healthy attitude, looking and feeling your best. If it is true that youth is wasted on the young, then mid-life and beyond should be savored.

You have a maintenance program for your house, car, and washing machine, right? Now you should know all the quick and easy secrets to provide the same "maintenance" to extend your youthful years. The trick is to figure out what your priorities and expectations are. This chapter tells you how to give yourself a face-lift at home, but it also tells you about the cosmetic surgery options that exist out there.

Cosmetic surgery isn't for everyone, and you don't have to be a millionaire to pay for any of the procedures outlined in this chapter. The latest research shows that 65 percent of people who undergo some form of cosmetic surgery have incomes under $50,000. But you should make sure that you know all the ins and outs of this technology.

You can amble through midlife the way your predecessors have, accepting the wrinkles, thinning hair, and thickening waist like trophies, or you can do it the *The Lazy Way,* by putting up your dukes and fighting this aging process with everything you've got!

KEEP YOUR CHIN UP!

Whether you give yourself an instant face-lift or find a great dermatologist, there are some amazingly simple ways to take some of the years off your face.

The Instant Face-Lift—Really!

You might think I'm kidding, but I'm not. At last you can learn the age-defying secrets of the stars. Do you need an instant tuck or lift in minutes? Believe it or not, by using a few special elastics and surgical tape, you can make some of those years seem to disappear! This device eliminates lines around the eyes and mouth and helps give smooth, firm control of the jawline and neck. First some basic tips, and then we'll get into the crucial stuff!

- Fresh tape should be used each time you decide to do an instant lift. If your skin becomes sensitive, wait a few days before continuing use.

- For extra hold, use Duo Surgical Adhesive, Duo Eyelash Adhesive, or any lash adhesive available.

YOU'LL THANK YOURSELF LATER

Accept the facts that prune juice tastes no worse than Kool-aid and that you can enjoy sex without Viagra. After all, a good sex life makes your skin glow, and you radiate energy and vitality!

Place a small drop of adhesive on the area where the tape will be placed.

■ Tap the adhesive lightly until it disappears, and then apply tape.

■ Apply makeup.

Instant Face-Lift

You'll need two pieces of hypoallergenic surgical tape attached to two 4-inch elastics, one of which has eyelets on it for adjusting tension. You can find the elastic at any costume store (they carry these for masks).

Getting Ready

1 Stand in front of the mirror and put your fingers in front of your ears. Pull back the skin until the area you want to deal with looks smooth and free of lines. Try the same in front of the neck and eye area. Wherever you decide to "lift" is where you'll place the tapes.

2 You'll be applying the tapes before you do your makeup, so you'll need to first cleanse designated areas with rubbing alcohol and make sure the area is free of makeup and oils. Prepare the lifts by placing the stemhook that is on the end of the elastic through the hole in the tapes. Do not remove the paper backing until you are ready to apply them to the skin.

3 To apply the tapes, remove the protective paper from the tape. Place the adhesive side against the skin in the desired area. Press firmly and rub gently for 10 seconds to assure good contact.

IF YOU'RE SO
INCLINED

Take a test run of the instant face-lift over the weekend, and you'll be walking with your head held high come Monday!

QUICK ⬭ PAINLESS

Little tendrils around the face are especially effective to cover tapes. Hairpieces, wigs, and scarves may also be useful for concealing the lifts.

Lifting the Nose to Mouth Lines

After preparing the area as described above, this is the next step to giving yourself a face-lift.

1 Separate the hair from the top of the ear to the back and top of the head. Comb the hair forward or pin it out of the way. Apply the tapes to both sides of the front of the ears and draw the elastics up while pulling the skin smoothly, but not so taut as to cause creases in the skin. Place the stemhook in the appropriate eyelet to obtain the desired tension. You can use a bobby pin to keep the elastics in place.

2 To smooth out your eye lines, use the same procedure as described in step one above, but you will apply the tapes to the temple area instead. You will find that you need to draw the elastics a little farther back on the head for this application.

Smooth Out Neck Lines

For this application, you will be using two shorter elastics than you used in the above lifts, and they should have a stemhook on both ends. There are two varieties of these shorter elastics, so experiment with both and find out which elastic gives you the desired result. I recommend that you start with the longer elastic first. The elastics used for the neck area are beige in color in order to blend with the skin. Brown neck elastics are also available.

1 Add a tape to each end, making sure the stemhook is on the outside—not against the skin.

2   Draw the skin back on one side and apply one tape below and slightly behind the ear lobe, drawing skin back on the other side and apply a second tape.

3   Do not remove the backing paper until you are ready to apply the tape. If you do not obtain the smoothness desired, try the shorter elastic.

Once you have applied your tapes for your instant face- or neck-lift, you can finish getting ready for your close-up! Comb your hair back in place, but use a little creative arranging to cover the lifts. Try creating little tendrils around the face to cover them—this is a highly effective technique! Hairpieces, wigs, and scarves can also be used to conceal your lifts.

A Good Dermatologist Can Go a Long Way

Have you always thought that a good facial, by definition, required hours of free time to spend at a spa or beauty clinic? Surprise! Facial peels, which can make your face as smooth as a baby's bottom, can be done on your lunch hour! That's right; it's called a "lunch-time peel." This procedure causes a minimum of reddening that can be covered up by makeup before returning to work. You will need two to four treatments spaced a week or two apart.

AGE DEFYING TECHNIQUES

Okay, so you've always wondered about cosmetic surgery and if it is really what you want to do. Well, it's definitely an option that can seriously erase some of those years. If

Congratulations! Before you made an appointment for a cosmetic procedure, you did your homework and got the best person for you! Treat yourself to a walk on the beach with a loved one.

The Lazy Way

you follow my tips and information, you can lie like a rug about your age and get away with it! Even when you shave off 10 years and say you are 40 when you are really 50, you will actually have people telling you how good you look for your age! Consider the following suggestions for the best possible skin care.

TAKING THE PLASTIC OPTION

I bet you have spent more money on home improvements than on yourself. Come on, fess up. It's okay, because you can do something about it now. Be aware, however, that since health insurance does not cover these surgical procedures, you will need to find a way to finance whichever treatment you choose.

A Cut Above the Rest

If you do decide to take the plunge and go for cosmetic surgery in any way, shape, or form, make sure you know what you're getting into. Forewarned is forearmed. Think about how picky you are when picking a new restaurant, hotel, or other service. You make sure that you will get the best for your dollar, right? And you're also checking to make sure that the service provider you're choosing has your best interests in mind, so why do any less when it comes to your appearance?

- Never pick a physician or facility based on an advertisement or article. The best sources for referrals are happy patients and physicians who care about the quality of their work.

YOU'LL THANK YOURSELF LATER

Afraid that things won't work out, and you'll end up looking like Attila the Hun? Ask the doctor what he or she would be willing to do at no charge? Find out any hidden costs for follow-up work up front.

- Get at least four referrals, read as much as you can, and discuss this procedure with those who can share their own experiences.

- Web site research is crucial! Various goverment websites (such as www.nysed.gov/home/regents.html in New York State) will tell you if the doctor you're considering is licensed. You can also call your state department of health to uncover any malpractice suits against the physician.

Be Aware!

If cosmetic surgery is the option you want, shop around first! Anyone about to perform cosmetic surgery must be board certified. This means that the doctor has completed medical school, an approved surgical residency of at least three years, two to three additional years of cosmetic surgery training, and has been in practice at least two years before passing a rigorous written and oral qualifying exam. Be wary of doctors claiming to be qualified cosmetic surgeons who are certified by obscure boards that are not recognized by the American Board of Medical Specialties.

TCA Peels

These are much safer than the more radical peels done with phenol that burn deep and carry the highest risk of infection and scarring.

Dermabrasion

This process gets rid of pockmarks, extensive sun damage, and deep lines above the lip. This technique is analogous to using sandpaper to smooth down a surface.

A COMPLETE WASTE OF TIME

The 3 Worst Things to Do When Considering Plastic Surgery:

1. Offer to be a guinea pig. If the doctor has not performed the operation you are seeking, exit stage right.

2. Rely on the "before-and-after" pictures to determine your choice of doctor.

3. After your "uplift," do all sorts of things that can undermine the results: for instance, overeating and being overexposed to the sun.

IF YOU'RE SO
INCLINED

A board-certified cosmetic surgeon has either had formal training in cosmetic surgery or in a given specialty (dermatology or ear, nose, and throat, for example) before taking the written and oral exams.

"Beam Me Up, Scotty!"—Laser Technology

Using lasers to smooth out your skin has become the hottest technique around. This is truly cutting-edge technology—a facial peel without chemicals, and considered "user friendly."

A continuous beam of light is emitted with short bursts, as the doctor circles your face. Some lasers are computerized to make sure there are no uneven surfaces on your skin. Be warned, however, that immediately after the treatment, you might look like you have gone a couple of rounds with Evander Holyfield. But don't worry! With the proper gels, antibiotic creams, and bandages, the skin will heal, and the pain will subside.

Collagen Injections

This is the easiest way to help stop wrinkling. This has been known to "plump" up the skin and is a quick procedure to fill in laugh lines and crow's feet around the eyes. The downside is that it only lasts three or four months.

Liposuction—Is It for You?

Flatten that pot belly and cinch in those love handles in one day! Feeling dumpy or hippy as well? This is definitely *The Lazy Way* to trimming the tummy, thighs, hips, and "love handles." In fact, this latest surgical procedure can get rid of two gallons of fat!

Getting Time on Your Side

	The Old Way	The Lazy Way
Weekly facials	1 hour	3 minutes
Thigh machine workout	30 minutes 3 times a week	1 hour once a week
Ab workouts	2 hours	15 minutes
Getting a face-lift	6 weeks	1 minute
Fixing your face	20 minutes	4 minutes
Erasing wrinkles	45 minutes	2 to 10 minutes

Part 2

Your Fast Track to Anti-Aging

Are you too lazy to read "Your Fast Track to Anti-Aging?"

1 Do you find yourself wondering if you'll ever be thin again? ☐ yes ☐ no

2 Do you ever feel as if you could never leave your house without a three-hour primping session? ☐ yes ☐ no

3 Do you get tired of looking tired? ☐ yes ☐ no

Testing—As Easy As 1-2-3

The moment of truth is here. But listen, before you start berating yourself for not exercising sooner, just remember that it's never too late! Now is the time to find out how fit you are. Do you really know what kind of shape you're in? How does your fitness level stack up against the rest of the population? Is it safe for you to exercise?

EVALUATE YOURSELF

To find the answers to these questions, take the tests in this chapter, either by yourself or with the help of a fitness buddy. Your scores will highlight your strengths and weaknesses, giving you a blueprint for your fitness program and goals.

Don't be surprised if your initial scores are lower than the median scores for "normal" test takers. It does not mean you can't be healthy and fit. Every 30 days you will need to test yourself again and record your scores alongside those from your first tests. Believe it or not, the differences will amaze you!

As with anything else, if you are in doubt about your health, check with a medical doctor before starting your testing or exercise program. Ready? On your mark, get set, go!

Getting to the Heart of the Matter

You won't need a lot of things to test yourself, but the few items you will need are pretty crucial. Here they are:

- Stool (eight inches high)
- Tennis shoes
- Tape measure
- Yardstick
- Stopwatch

First of all, everyone's cardiovascular capacity is unique. The answers to your exercise questions lie in your heart's capacity to meet the demands placed on it. To determine how your heart is functioning, you have to start out by learning how to take your pulse. This simple procedure will help you gauge your heart rate if you're resting and if you're exercising. By interpreting your heart rate, you will know your heart's capacity.

To find your pulse, you need to follow these guidelines:

1. Place three fingers lightly over the artery near the inside center of the wrist.

2. Move your fingertips around until you feel the pulse.

3. If you have trouble locating your pulse in your wrist,

Before going too far with these tests, recruit an exercise buddy. Having a personal cheering section is always great for the body and soul!

place two or three fingers along your neck about one inch below your jawbone.

4. Using a stopwatch or the second hand on a wristwatch or clock, count the number of pulses for 15 seconds. Multiply this number by four to get your heart rate in beats per minute.

Test 1: Find Your Resting Heart Rate

The first measurement you need is your resting heart rate. The best time to take it is when you wake up in the morning. If your resting heart rate is over 100 beats a

YOU'LL THANK YOURSELF LATER

Keep on top of your weight! If you are overweight and lack flexibility, you can't be very mobile, and your weight will decrease your cardiovascular fitness.

Resting Heart Rate Comparison

	20–29	30–39	40–49	50+
		Age		
		Men		
Excellent	59 or less	63 or less	65 or less	67 or less
Good	60–69	64–71	66–73	68–75
Fair	70–85	72–85	74–89	76–89
Poor	86+	86+	90+	90+
		Women		
Excellent	71 or less	71 or less	74 or less	76 or less
Good	72–77	72–79	75–79	77–83
Fair	78–95	80–97	80–98	84–102
Poor	96+	98+	99+	103+

minute, call your doctor immediately. Now write your resting heart rate into your Personal Fitness Profile.

The previous table shows what your resting heart rate should be by combining beats per minute, gender, and age. How do you rate?

Are You Aerobically Able?

The next thing you have to discover is how aerobically fit you are and how much stamina you have. This test reveals how fast your heart and lungs deliver oxygen to your body and how long it takes your pulse to slow down after it has been sped up through exercise. This test is important because it will tell you how strong your heart really is. It will also help you determine the effectiveness of your quick shape-up program. The sooner your heart returns to its resting rate, the better your condition. Ready? Just follow these simple steps.

Test 2: Maximum Heart Rate

This exercise gives you your maximum heart rate. If it is higher than those listed on the chart, consult a doctor before exercising aerobically.

1. Step on a chair or stool about eight inches high, and then step down again, moving one foot after the other. Repeat 24 times a minute for three minutes. Stop and take your pulse.

2. After resting for 30 seconds, take your pulse again and consult the chart. If you feel dizzy, nauseous, or painfully breathless, stop!

Congratulations! You've learned how to combat the aging of your heart! Reward yourself with a beautiful heart necklace or your favorite CD. You're being heart smart, and what could be better than that?

The Lazy Way

The following tables will help you get an idea of what your maximum heart rate is really telling you. Both tables are a good test to see just how fit your heart really is.

Safe Maximum Heart Rate

	20–29	Age 30–39	40–49	50+
Men	170	160	150	140
Women	170	160	150	140

Recovery Heart Rate at 30 Seconds

	20–29	Age 30–39	40–49	50+
Men				
Excellent	74	78	80	83
Good	75–84	79–86	81–88	84–90
Fair	85–101	87–101	89–105	91–105
Poor	102+	102+	106+	106+
Women				
Excellent	86	86	88	90
Good	87–93	87–94	89–94	91–98
Fair	94–111	95–113	95–114	99–117
Poor	112+	114+	115+	118+

WEIGHING IN

Are you still with me? Great! Now it's time to top off your testing program with finding out how much extra "stuff" you are carrying around on your body. If you want to be fit and fabulous, you must attack this problem area next. The best place to start, of course, is to find out what the correct weight for your height really is, and then see how you measure up.

Figuring Your Target Weight

In order to figure out what your target weight should be, you need to consider a few factors: gender, height, and age. The weights in the lower range generally apply to women because they tend to have less muscle and bone than men (sob, sob!). Higher weights apply to men (yea!!!!!). The weights in the following table is without clothes, and your height without shoes on.

Of course if you have the time, the most accurate method of determining your target weight is by looking at your body composition by using skin fold measurements and/or underwater weighing. Your target weight is calculated from your percentage of body fat vs. lean tissue (muscle). Generally, the percentage of body fat for men should not exceed 19 percent and for women, 23 percent.

Other Weighty Methods

As always, there is more than one way to skin a cat! Here's another to go about calculating your target weight:

IF YOU'RE SO INCLINED

A reliable health or fitness facility in your area can measure your body fat. You can try your local college. Consult with a health professional to identify your healthiest weight and body fat.

- For women, allow 100 pounds for the first 5 feet. For every inch over 5 feet, add 5 pounds. So if you are 5 feet 5, a rough target weight would be 125 pounds.

Target Weight Table

Height	Weight (lbs.)	
	Ages 19–34	Ages 35+
5'0"	97–128	108–138
5'1"	101–132	111–143
5'2"	104–137	115–148
5'3"	107–141	119–152
5'4"	111–146	122–157
5'5"	115–150	126–161
5'6"	118–155	130–167
5'7"	121–160	134–172
5'8"	125–164	138–178
5'9"	129–169	142–183
5'10"	132–174	146–188
5'11"	136–179	151–194
6'0"	140–184	155–199
6'1"	144–189	159–205
6'2"	148–195	164–210
6'3"	152–200	168–216
6'4"	156–205	179–222
6'5"	160–211	177–228
6'6"	164–216	183–234

■ For men, allow 106 pounds for the first 5 feet, and 6 pounds for every inch over 5 feet. So a man who is 6 feet tall would have a target weight of 178 pounds.

■ Add or subtract 10 percent for a large frame, respectively.

Counting Caloric Quotients

Just as each person has a unique target weight—depending on age, gender, and body type—everyone also has a specific caloric need. This will tell you what you may need to change in your diet, whether to incorporate more, or start cutting back. Either way, this is definitely something to stay on top of!

To figure out your caloric needs, find your age range in the chart below, and then multiply your current weight times the multiplying factor listed for your age group. If you are at the lower end of the age range and have more than one factor to choose from, then choose the lower number offered.

So, look at the chart carefully. If you are 45 years old and weigh 150 pounds, your baseline caloric need is 1,650 calories a day.

Caloric Need Table

Age Range	Multiplying Factor
20–29	13 to 15
30–39	12
40–49	11
50+	10

Test 3: Measuring Your Body Fat—The Pinch Test

There are various elaborate tests to measure your body composition, which will determine how much fat you are carrying. Fat can be measured with **calipers**. They look like those contraptions that the iceman uses to carry ice blocks. Or fat can be measured with underwater scales, but you really don't need to be a rocket scientist to decide if you are carrying too much fat. Just follow these easy instructions and try the pinch test.

1. Pinch yourself at the waist and upper arm.

2. Grab as much flesh as you can.

If you pinch about an inch, you're probably okay, but if you're nearer to the two- or three-inch mark, you'll need to work on toning down some of that body fat. Not only will you be on the road to a healthier you, you'll also look and feel terrific!

All right, the major testing is out of the way, but, just to make you fully aware of your fitness level, we really have to add another short test.

Test 4: Measuring Your Flexibility

This one will help you judge just how much your muscles, ligaments, and tendons have suffered from lack of use. Just follow these steps:

1. Make a starting line on the floor.

2. Sit on floor with legs outstretched, feet six inches apart and heels touching the line.

3. Place a yardstick between your legs, perpendicular to the starting line, with the 15-inch mark at the

QUICK ✦ PAINLESS

Yep, you get to choose how to lose by the following methods! Since a pound equals 3,500 calories, you can:

▪ Cut 500 calories per day to lose 1 pound a week.

▪ Cut 250 calories per day to lose 1/2 pound per week.

▪ Walk 2 1/2 miles in 37 minutes or jog it in 25 minutes to burn 250 calories a day and lose 1/2 pound a week!

▪ Combine cutting calories and exercise for maximum results.

Congratulations! You did it. Now grab your television clicker, hop onto your couch, and watch your favorite show. You deserve it!

The Lazy Way

line. Keep your heels on the line and your legs straight.

4. With your hands stretched in front of you, slowly bend forward without straining or bouncing and touch the yardstick.

5. Note the measurement on the yardstick. Measure the space between your starting line (15 on the yardstick) and where your fingertips reached the yardstick. Score a plus figure if you are able to touch behind the heel and a minus figure if you are not able to reach that far.

Flexibility Stretch Rating (Measurements Are in Centimeters)

	Up to 35	Age 36–45	46+
		Men	
Excellent	+6	+5	+4
Good	-3	+2	+1
Fair	-5	-5	-6
Poor	-8	-10	-10
		Women	
Excellent	+8	+7	+6
Good	+5	+4	+3
Fair	-1	-3	-2
Poor	-4	-5	-6

Your Endurance and Strength Tests

Endurance is a basic element of physical fitness. To maintain aerobic fitness, you need to sustain muscular effort without fatigue. Strength is necessary for you to healthfully participate in some form of recreational sport.

Test 5: The Sit-Up Test

1. Lie on your back with your ankles firmly planted beneath a solid object or held by another person.

2. Put your hands behind your head, and with knees bent, pull yourself up to a sitting position, using the strength of your stomach muscles.

3. See how many sit-ups you can manage within 60 seconds, and consult the following chart to measure your result.

Test That Torso!

Now for the grand finale! Let's see how strong your upper body is. Men usually do very well with push-ups, while many women lack the strength in their upper bodies to repeatedly perform them. Nevertheless, this test can help determine your overall body strength.

Test 6: The Upper Body Strength Test

1. For men: Start in a front-leaning position, supporting your body by bending at the elbows until your chest touches the floor. Keep your body flat and rigid.

Congratulations! You've set yourself an honorable goal: to determine if your existing strength and muscular endurance are adequate to keep up with everyday living and leisure activities. Treat yourself to an afternoon with the family!

The Lazy Way

2. For women: Start with your knees bent, in a front leaning position, and support your body by bending at the elbows until your chest touches the floor.

3. Return to starting position.

Your score is the number of correct, complete push-ups you can do. But ladies, don't worry if your score is

Muscular Endurance

		Endurance Rating	
Age	Excellent	Good	Poor
		Men	
12–14	45	35	25
15–19	50	40	30
20–29	40	30	20
30–39	35	25	20
40–49	30	20	15
50–59	25	15	10
60–69	23	13	8
		Women	
12–14	44	34	24
15–19	40	30	20
20–29	33	23	13
30–39	27	17	12
40–49	22	12	7
50–59	20	10	5
60–69	17	7	4

low. You can include strength exercises for this area of your body when you set up your personal fitness program. So, how did you do?

These tests are really easy to do and can give you an excellent idea of your fitness level. Make sure you go through these honestly and accurately. And no fudging! It won't help anyone, especially yourself, if you're not honest about how you did on these tests!

Now that you've started on the right track to becoming a fitter, healthier you, try to incorporate a few of these tips into your new lifestyle. You'll be glad you did it!

These tips are to help you stay on top of your progress:

- Re-evaluate your fitness level every 30 days
- Keep your Personal Fitness Profile record current
- Set realistic goals and remember that it's all about progress and not perfection

A COMPLETE WASTE OF TIME

The 3 Worst Ways You Can Do Your Push-Ups, Sit-Ups, and Stretching Tests Are:

1. Push-up test: letting your chest touch ground first.

2. Sit-up test: forcing your head up first.

3. Stretching test: bending your knees.

Muscular Strength and Endurance Standards for Adult Men and Women

	Sit-Ups (60 seconds)	Push-Ups (Front-leaning position)
Excellent	30 or more	15 or more
Good	25–29	10–14
Fair	20–24	5–9
Poor	Fewer than 20	Fewer than 5

TAKE CARE OF YOURSELF!

There are a few things everyone should do for himself or herself, no matter how healthy you think you are, or how well you did on the tests in this chapter. If you scored well on these evaluators, I congratulate you! But that doesn't mean that you can slack off now on making sure everything is in tip-top shape. You owe it to yourself to be as healthy as you can be!

Talk to your physician about having these evaluations done:

- If you are over 35, you should have a medical evaluation incorporating a 12-lead electrocardiogram and blood pressure test.

- Get a blood profile and body composition test as additional helpful measures.

- You should have at least a five-hour blood glucose tolerance test and liver enzyme test.

Congratulations! Now that you know what level you are at, you have the necessary information and motivation to set up your very own fitness program. Treat yourself to an afternoon of pampering! You deserve it!

The Lazy Way

Getting Time on Your Side

	The Old Way	The Lazy Way
Taking body fat measurements	3 hours	1 minutes
Fitness testing	1/2 day	20 minutes
Melting 5 pounds	3 hours	30 minutes
Finding out if you are aerobically able	3 hours	5 minutes
Creating the right fitness program for you	Where do I start?	An afternoon
Knowing which evaluations you need from your doctor and when to get them done	Where do I start?	2 minutes

Chapter four

Easy Steps to Becoming an Ageless Wonder

Now that you've completed your self-evaluation and fitness tests and received approval from your doctor, you are ready to start exercising. By the time you finish this chapter, you will be walking and jogging regularly, and will be ready to start weight training and recreational sports.

ADULTS ONLY: HOW THE BODY AGES

Does all this sound too good to be true? Well, it's not; you can do it! How is this possible, you say? Well, I want to devote an itty-bitty section here to jog your memory as to how your body ages. Armed with the information from this book, you'll experience only 20 percent of the biomarkers of the aging process. Let's start with just the facts. Keep in mind that the information in this list is telling you about the average aging process, but there are ways to fight these biomarkers, so take heart!

■ **Mental Functions.** By age 60, 45 percent of your brain cells will have died. Not to worry, though; you still have

more than enough gray matter to read about the
Clinton scandal or even become a champion chess
player or take up a foreign language. You will, however, notice the symptoms of DRAFT: Don't
Remember A Friggin' Thing! But don't worry, be
happy, because all that really means is that it's just
taking you longer to process the info from your
memory bank.

Sleep and Aging. As we age, deep, slow, and
restorative sleep declines, with an increase of bathroom visits after age 50; this is due to a swollen
prostate for men and a prolapsed bladder for
women.

Muscles and Bones. By age 45, the strength starts to
wane. By 55, a man's grip is 70 percent of what it
was at age 25. From 40 years young and on, we lose
bone faster than we make it; we experience osteoporosis from vertebrae compression. Amazingly
enough, women will actually lose inches in height—
at least two inches—as they age because of this
compression.

Sex. Read it and don't weep! Research indicates that
the frequency of sex diminishes from three times a
week for 20-year-old married men to one and a half
times a week for married men in their 50s. While it
can take 20 minutes for a 20-year-old to go a second
round, it might take his older counterpart as long as
12 hours! If you are a smoker, this particular problem becomes bleaker. Well, guys, there's always
Viagra! And ladies, have I got good news for you!

By using estrogen replacements, you can battle the diminishment of your sex drive.

- **Joints.** You've all heard it, that creaking sound coming from the depths of all your bendy places. This is because joints have a limited life span, and most doctors will not replace them before you hit the age of 60. So cut down on the high-impact athletics for a while, take up yoga, and moderate your aerobic activities.

- **Skin.** Women, it's not gravity here that's your enemy, but the skin losing its elasticity. Men aren't hit as hard here, although they will develop liver and age spots.

- **Weight.** Somewhere between age 40 and 70, women will pack on an extra 15 pounds—usually in the hip area—while men will notice their "love handles" becoming more prominent.

- **Heart.** The older you get, the slower your heart will pump, but it will deliver more blood to the heart chamber with more efficiency. Oxygen use will decline about 10 percent every 10 years.

- **Eyes.** Ever wonder why you can only read a menu when you have it stretched out in front of you? It's because the lens in your eye has started to harden. It all starts with buying magnifiers, and then you go in for glasses. But technology has given us the gift of laser surgery, so check it out; if your sight problem can be corrected with this procedure, you can "trash" your glasses!

YOU'LL THANK YOURSELF LATER

Keep track of your weight! It's the key to keeping yourself fit and happy!

Some corporations have fitness lunch breaks to encourage employee well-being, because they know that the payoffs are worth the investment. A fit employee is more productive, requires fewer sick leaves, and has a positive mental attitude.

Well, the information you just read certainly should have motivated you to get a hitch in your gidalong and start working to reverse the aging process. But before you pull on your sweats and lace up your shoes, prepare your mind for the challenge ahead. Some of you will be asking yourselves a lot of questions. The answers that follow will ensure confidence and success.

WHEN TO GET YOUR GROOVE ON

Not sure when you should exercise or even why you should? Different times of the day carry with them secret rewards, so take a look at the following lists and see what time of day will benefit you the most!

Morning exercise will give you the following benefits, so take some time to consider this option:

- You will have cleared your mind for the day's pressures and pleasures.

- You will begin your day knowing you have succeeded in completing a workout. Even if it's just my Housercise workout that I describe in Chapter 5. This feeling will carry you through the day and result in improved performance and a sense of self-esteem.

Exercising in the afternoon will let you reap the following rewards:

- You will have cleared the stress and anxiety that have built up in the morning.

- It is easier to find others to join you.

If you prefer to work out in the evening, be sure your exercise schedule does not conflict with an activity you consider a major priority. The benefits from evening workouts include:

- The chance to get rid of the stress, anxiety, anger, and frustration that may have built up during the day.

- The option of choosing a health club over a bar for unwinding after a hard day.

- When you exercise in the evening, you avoid the opportunity to soothe your feelings with food. Instead of stuffing your feelings, you drain off the negativity and enjoy the rewards of positive behavior.

When deciding when to exercise, carefully consider what are the things that make it hard you to stick to it. If it's harder to get your motor started in the morning, a morning workout may be just the ticket! If you feel that having an exercise buddy is necessary, an afternoon session is just what the doctor ordered. If you find yourself eating your way out of a stressful day when you've left work, an evening workout time will help you stay focused, healthy, and out of the fridge!

WORKING OUT MADE SIMPLE

You don't have to spend hundreds of dollars on gym subscriptions or exercise equipment to have a successful exercise routine. Your workout room could be as close as your basement or just outside the front door!

- You can work out at your home—outside or inside. By following the beginner's program in this book, you will slowly start to get in shape by walking or jogging in your neighborhood or at a nearby park or school track.

Congratulations! You've found time to exercise! Treat yourself to a new CD to make those workouts boogie!

The Lazy Way

You can even set up your own home gym in your basement, den, or extra space. Home exercise equipment has become popular and is available at many price levels and styles. The idea is to figure out what goals you are trying to achieve, how much you want to spend, and the amount of space you need to allocate.

Before you go shopping, consider every angle and remind yourself what you are trying to accomplish. Rome was not built in one day! Don't shop for everything at once, and don't be fooled by those salespeople who will try to sell you the "Ultimate Exercise Machine Guaranteed to Make You into a Bodybuilder in Two Days." Those machines don't exist, so save your money and your self-esteem!

To-Do List

Every great success story starts out with a well-considered plan! Use this to-do list to maximize your exercise experience. When you go to press the incline button on your treadmill, you don't want to hit your head on the ceiling or your fancy chandelier; so first you'll need to take measurements, and then it's time to find the best place to put it all.

- Take measurements (not yours, silly!)
    - Length, width, and height of space you have chosen
    - Measure doors to make sure you can get the piece of equipment through

- Choose the best location for your equipment
    - Put stationary bike in front of the TV, stereo, or even a window
    - Keep all equipment in close proximity
    - Make sure your chosen spot is well ventilated

Compare, Compare, Compare!

Remember that song, "You Better Shop Around?" Here are some great guidelines to follow to stretch your dollar:

- Stick with outlets that specialize in the equipment you're going to use.

- Knowing the exact make and model of a piece of equipment will clear the way for you to deal directly with the manufacturer and eliminate the costs of dealing with the "middle man."

- Buy used equipment, but make sure it includes a trial period and instruction manuals.

- I can't emphasize this one enough: be sure you test every item before lugging it home!

Here are some more useful tips to keep in mind before you sign on the dotted line:

- Ask for a 10 percent discount because most items are marked up.

- Buying several items? Ask for a complimentary item such as a floor mat to place your equipment on. This prevents indents in carpets and keeps them clean. They can run as much as $200 if bought separately.

QUICK PAINLESS

It only takes a second to make a few calls ahead of time. So, let your fingers do the walking so you don't have to!

IF YOU'RE SO
INCLINED

Check with the Better
Business Bureau before
making an investment.
Odds are, you'll thank
yourself later!

Stick with a one-year warranty on any item you consider purchasing.

Find out who can repair your equipment if it breaks down. Make sure that the repair service isn't 2,000 miles away!

As with any major purchase, be wary of being ripped off. These warnings should be taken very seriously:

Machines that promise you that you can tone muscles without exercising? Hello! These belong in the land of fairy tales because they sure don't exist on this planet!

Never buy from a celebrity endorser who hasn't been seen in the last five years. Be very leery of someone with a perfect body hawking some contraption that looks like it came from another planet. Trust me, they did not use it to create the shape they are in.

"Three Easy Payments." Do you really want to know what that means? "Actual Cost $80." Yeah, right! Three payments of $25.95, plus adding in shipping and handling, and you're back up to the cost of the pre-sale price!

"Not Sold in Stores." This is a popular sales ploy used to create a sense of urgency in you, the unsuspecting buyer. After a few months, I guarantee that you'll see the item sold in stores, so don't get sucked in by this one!

Don't be swayed by new anti-aging scientific terminology. These words are thrown around to lull you into buying the product being pitched. Believe it or not, some terms have been proven to not even exist!

TRUE VALUE

Hold it! Are you really thinking about spending $100 for a pair of tennis shoes, $30 on a jog bra or jock strap, and another $30 on kneepads? Right about now I bet your only liquid asset is a bottle of Gatorade! But don't fret; listed next are fitness items to die for, all under $50!

Insane Deals

You'd be crazy if you didn't at least consider some of these trusty exercise companions!

- **Body bar.** This acts as a dumbbell without the bells, it weighs in anywhere from 9 to 36 pounds, and works arms, shoulders, chest, legs, and abs. This is good for a whole body workout! This little wonder goes for $40 and up.

- **Radio/tape player.** Clip this onto your shorts or sweats, or place in a sweat proof pouch that wraps around your waist, and you'll be boogying right on through! As little as $40.

- **Clear water bottle.** Gotta keep up on those fluids! You can buy this for as little as $5.

- **Oversized plastic ball.** This is used to improve the flexibility of the lower back: $30.

- **Exercise videos.** There are literally hundreds of 30-minute tapes from $9.95 to $14.95.

- **Prostretch.** This will stretch those calf and shin muscles and the sides of your ankles: $25.

YOU'LL THANK YOURSELF LATER

Hide your credit card from 10 p.m. until 7 a.m. Turn off the boob tube and go to bed. Eliminate the temptation of the shopping networks!

QUICK ⬭ PAINLESS

If you keep one bag of workout stuff in your car, one at home, and one at the office, you'll be ready to stroll whenever time allows!

■ **PowerBelt.** Works arms, shoulders, back, and chest. You pull on handles attached to a waist pack, and the disks inside the belt provide resistance. It's good for adding an upper-body workout, allowing you to burn more calories: $49.95.

■ **Jump rope.** Get one with soft foam or rubber handles—a great calorie burner! The deluxe type goes for $30 tops.

PACKING CHEAP FOR HOME, GYM, OR OFFICE

You don't need to buy an entire wardrobe to accommodate your new fitness lifestyle, believe me! Just make sure you have these few simple items, and you'll be ready to go!

■ Pair of standard tennis shoes

■ Wool or cotton socks

■ Nylon shorts for summer, cotton for colder weather

■ Baggy sweats for really cold weather

STRETCH YOURSELF FIT

Now that you have all the accoutrements to start your conditioning program and you have made your "appointment" with yourself, you are ready to begin your aerobic walking program. Remember, you can accomplish your goal even if you want to go window shopping. But there is one thing you need to do before and after you stroll: stretching exercises. It's going to take you only a few minutes, and it's the best way to prevent pulled muscles and achy moments! You should consider your stretching routine to be as important a part of your fitness routine as the exercise, so don't cheat on this one!

- **Toe Touches.** Stretch very slowly by first reaching your arms high into the sky, and then bending slowly from the waist toward the ground. Keep your knees straight, and your heels flat on the floor. Don't worry if your fingers barely reach past your knees. Those muscles may not have been stretched for a long time, but eventually you will be able to stretch all the way down, really! Just stay relaxed, let your arms hang toward your feet, then stretch back up slowly, reaching toward the sky. Repeat five times.

- **Side Bends.** Stretch both arms into the air and interlace your fingers, with your palms facing the ceiling. Keeping your torso forward, stretch to the right of the waist. Stretch upright, and then to the left. Repeat five times for each side.

- **Wall Stretches.** Place your palms against the wall and lean in. Stretch your left arm back, keeping it straight, while bending your right leg. Push your body away from the wall. Hold the stretch, and then relax. Repeat five times. Alternate arms and legs, and repeat the stretch five times.

- **The Crunch.** This is a good ab workout. Just lie on your back with your legs on top of a bench or a

YOU'LL THANK YOURSELF LATER

Stretch, stretch, stretch! You can't get anything good out of abused muscles, so treat them right from the very start!

chair. Place your hands behind your head. Slowly lift your back 8 inches off the floor. Hold this position for two seconds, and then come back down slowly. Repeat five times.

Shake out your limbs, stretch a couple of more times, and you're ready to take a stroll! At the end of every walk, cool down by repeating your stretching routine to help work those fatigued and tight muscles. A proper warm-up and cool-down routine are essential to preventing injury and getting the most benefit from your workout.

IT ALL STARTS WITH A SINGLE STEP

The secret to all your endeavors is progress, not perfection. Follow the exercise prescription I have designed for you, and you'll immediately feel your life and body dramatically change.

- **Week One.** Once a day, three days per week, walk a distance of $1/2$ mile in 10 minutes. You will be walking at a rate of about three miles per hour.

- **Week Two.** Once a day, three days per week, walk a distance of one mile in 20 minutes.

- **Week Three.** Once a day, three days a week, walk a distance of $1^1/2$ miles in 30 minutes.

- **Week Four.** Once a day, three days per week, jog one-quarter mile, walk one-half mile, jog one-quarter mile.

IF YOU'RE SO
INCLINED

By now you might be getting a little bored and probably want more of a challenge. This means it's time to start jogging. If you don't feel quite ready to run, then continue increasing your walking mileage a $1/2$ mile every two weeks.

Keeping It Going

Once you begin running, you will probably notice that you have a distinctive running style. Think about what you do with your arms, hands, feet, legs, and breathing as you trot down the road. Do you feel constricted? Do you find yourself tensing up? If you do, it's time to rethink how you run.

To maximize your benefits, you'll need to teach yourself to run with a heel-first action, and push off on the ball of your foot with each stride. Start with short strides, lengthening as you progress. Concentrate on keeping your arms relaxed, and curl your fingers into loose fists; this will help you maintain good form while running. It is very important to keep your body straight and relaxed, so think about your breathing! Breathe rhythmically, and never hold your breath as you run!

Congratulations! You've incorporated a fabulous aerobic fitness program into your life, so schedule a 30-minute session once a week with a masseuse, and be proud of yourself! You just shaved 20 years off your life!

The Lazy Way

Getting Time on Your Side

	The Old Way	The Lazy Way
Daily workouts	1 1/2 hours	25 minutes
Unwinding after a hard day	3 hours	20 minutes
Muscle fatigue and recovery	3 days	30 minutes
Finding the right time to exercise for you	Never	It's easy!
Enjoying your workout	Ow!	That felt great!
Feeling energetic	It's been years!	Every day!

The Quickie 10-Minute Workout

As I've mentioned before, my schedule is more than hectic. But I know that I'm not alone when it comes to a hectic lifestyle. You probably have full-time jobs, take care of children, and manage a household. With your busy schedule, you probably don't have the opportunity to visit your local gym or health club for a daily workout. Does this mean you have no opportunity to improve yourself? No!

The good news is that no matter how busy you are, there are ways to get everything done and still be able to get some exercise in as well. You can kill two birds with one stone. All you have to do is perform my home fitness routine, a.k.a. "housercise." With a busy, full life, you need to get really creative when it comes to developing your own fitness routine.

Let's take an example from my own life: my business is service oriented, and often I don't have time to attend to my physical needs. To stay on track, I have had to come up with a home routine that addresses my physical fitness needs and gets my work done at the same time. When I find my time is crunched, I resort to housercise.

All you have to do is adapt your cleaning regime with a renewed attitude. After all, this system will let you work out and do your cleaning chores at the same time. Following are some of the items you'll need.

For the cleaning part of the job:

- Broom
- Mop
- Sponge(s)
- Vacuum cleaner
- Laundry basket
- Lawn rake
- Power lawn mower
- Snow shovel

For the exercise part of the job:

- Wrist and ankle weights
- Plastic juice jugs
- Chair
- Coffee table

As with any exercise session, don't forget to warm up before you start and cool down when you're done by stretching your muscles. So what if you can't touch your toes—or even see your toes—right now; we'll soon take care of that!

YOU'LL THANK YOURSELF LATER

Keep in mind that one does not have to race through my housercise routine sweating profusely. Research has shown that low-intensity aerobics are actually more effective in burning stored fat than short, high-intensity routines.

TWIST THAT TORSO

I like to call this my "Twist and Shout!" routine. It's a lot of fun, so don't just stand there—grab a broom and start twisting!

1. Hold the broomstick across the back of your shoulders. Spread your arms out wide and bend your knees slightly, while planting your feet firmly. Twist just at the waist, but do this slowly to prevent any spinal trouble.

2. Look straight ahead the entire time, and don't let your hips move. Because this exercise is just to get your juices flowing and there is no great resistance, focus on keeping your waist tight throughout each repetition. This exercise will take you only 60 seconds.

3. Now for the cleaning part. Sweep or mop as fast as possible. (Raking leaves can be applied to this workout as well.)

MOP 'N' TONE YOUR CHEST, ARMS, AND BACK

Whether you're a skinny-minnie or a chubby, to tone up and get firmness, shape, and strength in your arms, the following workouts will achieve quick results. Luckily, arms respond better to resistance exercises than any other body part does.

Believe it or not, it doesn't require much effort to reshape your arms. If you're out of shape, chances are

QUICK 🕮 PAINLESS

The only piece of advice to help you speed up results while you're twisting is to throw in a little extra va voom!

your arms are skinny and tire easily—even if you carry a sack of groceries half a block.

So let's be honest, are your arms skinny like Olive Oyl's, or are they meatier like Brutus's? If you're overweight, you're storing fat in your triceps. Genetically, men store more fat in their waistline and women store more fat in the backs of their arms. This can get out of hand, so take control!

Mop and Glow!

Now that you got yourself started by twisting away with your broom, grab that mop and get ready to clean yourself fit!

1. Place one hand on the end of the mop, the other near the neck, and press the mop firmly to the floor.

2. Mop to the right, left, and center. You can use the mop on walls, too.

Rub 'n' Scrub

The best exercises for toning up involve repetitive motions with the same set of muscles, so try this one on for size. You can work this in next time you wash your car, too.

1. Grab a sponge in each hand while cleaning the floor, kitchen counter, or any tabletop. Close your eyes and pretend you're the Karate Kid.

2. "Wipe on, wipe off." Move your arms in circles, one going toward you—"wipe on"—and one going away from you—"wipe off." Then circle both toward you and then away from you. Press hard!

Congratulations! You've gotten yourself into a great housercise routine! Now go to your icebox, grab your fat-free yogurt, and pig out! You earned it.

The Lazy Way

IT'S TIME TO PUMP YOU UP!

If you want to create a great shoulder line while firming up your chest and toning the front of your upper arms, these exercises were tailor-made for you!

Simple One-Arm Rows (Front Shoulder, Upper Back)

All you need for this one is yourself, a juice jug, and a chair. What could be easier than that? Try this one out when you're waiting for something to boil on the stove.

1. Get your chair and place your hand on the top for support. Position your body in a comfortable stance with your knees bent and your back in a neutral position.

2. Begin the movement with your weighted arm in a stretched position. Slowly pull the object up, keeping your arm close to your side.

3. When the "weight" reaches chest level, slowly return your arm to its original position and repeat. Try two or three sets of five to seven reps per arm.

Pump Up with Juice Jugs

This exercise is really effective, and you can do it while you're unloading your groceries! I recommend juice jugs for this, but any pair of relatively heavy grocery items—for example, two family size soup cans—will do just as nicely.

1. Grab two filled plastic juice jugs.

2. Stand in a comfortable position with your feet shoulder width apart.

YOU'LL THANK YOURSELF LATER

Despite your condition, don't give up the good fight. If you're not happy with your current condition, you haven't exercised, and you live on potato chips, then turn off the clicker, get off your tush, and do something about it before you have some kind of physical melt-down!

---

3. Hold the jugs with both hands, keeping them slightly apart from each other in front of your body. Slowly raise the jugs to your chin, keeping your elbows high and pointed out.

4. Return the jugs to the starting position and repeat.

BRING YOUR BOTTOM UP TO BEAR!

Most of my clients are locked into a frustrating battle to slim, shape, and firm their thighs, hips, and glutes. It's frustrating for me, too, because I know that heredity sometimes overrides everything—even physiological logic! But I also know that most people don't know the correct way to streamline their workouts to overcome this figure fault. This is where my information is invaluable. I have already learned that it can be done, so now it's time for you and me to do it together!

Vacuum and Firm Your Hips, Glutes, and Thighs the Easy Way

Vacuuming is a great housercise chore because the machine gives you some great resistance to work with, and it doesn't require you to buy any special exercise equipment!

1. As you push the vacuum forward, keep your body straight and step forward about four feet with your right foot. With your left leg held straight, slowly bend your right leg as much as possible.

2. At the bottom of the movement, your right knee should be several inches in front of your left ankle. You should feel a stretching in your thigh muscles.

IF YOU'RE SO
INCLINED

If you have to pick up items on the floor such as dog or cat toys, grandchildren's toys, or magazines, grab the laundry basket, fill it, and use that chore for your "lift and load" session of your housercise!

3. Slowly straighten your right leg and push back to your starting position. Now just alternate, whizzing around and cleaning your rooms!

Lift and Load—More Butt Firmers

We lift things all the time, but do we do it right? Make sure your knees do the work, not your back! And because you're lifting already, take a few extra moments and introduce this into your housercise routine by doing a couple of repetitions!

1. Bend over, grabbing the sides of a laundry basket. Squat, feet apart, toes diagonal.

2. Lift—but keep that back straight—and load (or unload).

WORK THOSE ABS!

After a bit of housercise, you'll probably want to rest. But what if I told you to go ahead? Shocked? Don't be! You can firm your abs at the same time! They cannot be overlooked.

My theory for ab training is very simple: don't be a counter, be a clock watcher! I use a clock and do as many ab exercises as I can in a short period of time while trying to keep good form throughout. If you can only work your abs for two minutes to start, that's okay, but keep in mind that you'll eventually want to work up to a four-minute ab workout.

YOU'LL THANK YOURSELF LATER

Abs quickly reoxygenate themselves and need constant tension to produce change. This means you should feel the "burn" while doing them. Take shorter rest periods between sets to keep your abs from reoxygenating.

Standard Ab Crunches

This exercise is made up of standard ab crunches, so it's pretty simple, but don't let its simplicity fool you! This is a crucial exercise!

1. Lie on your back, raise your knees, keeping your feet on the floor, while your hands are laced gently behind your head. Find a point on the ceiling and lift your shoulders off the floor as if you were trying to reach that point with your chest. Never pull the back of your head forward during the crunch, and don't allow your feet to leave the floor.

2. Take short rests, only until you feel a slight "burn," and continue—two minutes max. Try the same exercise with your feet on top of the couch instead of the floor.

Do these household chores, three times a week or more, for just 10 minutes (includes stretch time). You'll feel great and have a spotless home! You'll also get faster results by adding ankle weights and wrist weights to all your activities.

A COMPLETE WASTE OF TIME

The 3 Worst Ways You Can Work Your Abs:

1. Keeping legs straight when performing sit-ups. You'll use only 10 percent of your abdominal muscles.

2. Eating before you do your housercise, thinking you'll work it off.

3. Talking on the telephone while housercising. I didn't mention "mouthercise" for a reason!

Getting Time on Your Side

	The Old Way	The Lazy Way
Calories burned per hour by sweeping	150	300
Calories burned per hour by mopping	175	350
Calories burned per hour by doing laundry	100	200
Calories burned per hour by stair climbing	125	350
Calories burned per hour by raking the lawn	225	375
Calories burned per hour by shoveling snow	275	500

Part 3

Feeling and Looking Fit, Flabu-less, and Young

Are you too lazy to read "Feeling and Looking Fit, Flabu-less, and Young?"

1 Does your waistline doggedly resist every attempt at firming? ☐ yes ☐ no

2 Would you rather have a week in Paris but fear that you need that money to have Liposuction instead? ☐ yes ☐ no

3 Is your skin starting to dry out and crack like mud in a desert? ☐ yes ☐ no

Guilt-Free Eating in a Jiffy

I know that finding the time to eat—somewhere between squeezing 12 hours of work into an eight-hour day and attending to your social and family obligations—often means eating a meal or two on the run. Well, don't worry, because you're just one of the millions of Americans who grab a bite to eat at America's greatest contribution to the world of culinary cuisine: the fast-food restaurant.

Most people feel that healthy fast food is an oxymoron because few of the available choices seem to make up a healthy meal. We all know that there are some real diet busters out there. For example, Jack-In-The-Box's new "Colossus Burger" is two quarter-pound patties of beef, with three slices of cheese, eight pieces of bacon, and dressing—all adding up to 75 grams of fat. This one meal will have you exceeding your recommended intake of fat for the entire day! But what about some "healthy" foods, like chicken or fish, that may have been fried? Are they off-limits as well?

Well, here's the good news. If you search carefully, you can treat yourself to tasty, healthy, fat-free meals. I've put together a list of some of those choices and the nutritional breakdown of recommended foods such as chicken and fish.

Here's a guilt-free fast-food choice list for you.

Guilt-Free Fast Foods

Restaurant	Item	Fat grams	Calories	% Fat
Shoney's	Spaghetti	16	496	30
McDonald's	McLean Deluxe	10	320	28
Roy Rogers	Roast Beef	10	317	28
Wendy's	Large Chili	9	290	28
Shakey's	$1/10$ 12" Cheese Pizza (Thick Crust)	5	170	25
Subway	6" Turkey Sub	8	312	23
Burger King	Chunkey Chicken Salad	4	142	23
McDonald's	Chicken Salad	4	150	22
Domino's	2 slices 12" Cheese Pizza	6	340	16
Wendy's	Baked Potato (Sour Cream/Chives)	6	370	15
Jack-In-The-Box	Chicken Teriyaki Bowl	1.5	580	2

Get in the Know!

It's easy to find out what you're really eating—all you have to do is ask for a nutritional information brochure! Almost every fast-food restaurant out there provides them, from McDonald's to Carl Jr.'s.

STOCKING UP YOUR FREEZER

You don't have to go out to have a quick 'n' lazy meal; there are some great frozen meals out there that afford you great efficiency while staying low-fat! I have included a sample of the healthy frozen foods that are out there to get you started on choosing between what's good for you and what isn't. Please note that the following list is not comprehensive and is not an endorsement for any product.

But beware! Frozen dinners and entrees typically fall short of fiber and vitamins A and C. Calories can also be too few to sustain even a modest appetite. But don't fret! Here are a few ways you can supplement the nutrient makeup of any frozen meal:

- Add broiled tomatoes with garlic and Parmesan cheese, a crusty whole-grain roll, and orange slices.
- Add a spinach salad with lemon and low-calorie vinaigrette, a slice of whole-grain bread, and steamed carrots.

JUST SAY CHEESE!

With so many low-fat cheeses out there, you don't have to ignore this tasty treat anymore! Gone are the days

QUICK ⊙ PAINLESS

Every restaurant has a salad bar, so choose a fresh, green salad with low-cal dressing. Skip the fattening extras like cheeses and deli salads, which are often made with mayonnaise. One ounce of wine vinegar dressing has less than one gram of fat, while the same amount of blue cheese can contain 19 grams of fat—as much as some burgers.

Healthy Frozen Food Choices

Product	Calories	Fat	% Fat	Cholesterol (mg)	Sodium (mg)
Banquet—Healthy Balance					
Chicken Enchilada	300	4	4	15	630
Chicken Mesquite	310	9	26	45	800
Budget Gourmet—Light & Healthy					
Orange Glazed Chicken	290	3	9	25	800
Ham and Asparagus Au Gratin	300	14	42	50	860
Healthy Choice					
Mesquite Chicken	340	1	3	45	290
Chicken Enchilada	310	9	26	35	480
Le Menu Healthy—Light Style					
Veal Marsala	230	3	12	75	700
Salisbury Steak	280	9	29	35	400
Stouffer's Lean Cuisine Entrees					
Chicken a L'Orange	280	4	13	55	290
Baked Cheese Ravioli	240	8	30	55	590
Weight Watchers					
Chicken Polynesian	190	1	5	20	240
Southern Baked Chicken	170	7	37	45	520

when lunch for a calorie conscious person had to consist of just a bowl of plain cottage cheese. Check out some of these ideas:

- Nonfat cottage cheese is boring no more! Just add a fresh, juicy tomato for great flavor and super vitamins, or mix in some fruit for a sweet and healthy breakfast!

- Try the Italian version of nonfat ricotta for a breakfast treat by mixing equal portions of nonfat ricotta and unsweetened applesauce, along with a sprinkle of cinnamon, to top a toasted English muffin.

In the past, high-fat cheese has been the downfall of homemade pizza. But now you can have your pizza—hold the pepperoni—and your physique, too! Cheese makers like Healthy Choice, Kraft, Sargento, and others make pizza preparation easier with shredded mozzarella and pizza cheese combos. Healthy Choice even has terrific garlic-flavored shreds. These shredded and grated cheese products offer convenience and easier portion control—just rememeber: one serving equals ¼ cup!

HOME GROWN—ORGANICALLY SPEAKING!

Another great way to eat without feeling guilty is to indulge in natural organic foods. Organic means that a product was grown and processed without toxic pesticides, herbicides, fungicides, or chemical fertilizers. Organic foods are low in fat and nutrient dense.

IF YOU'RE SO
INCLINED

Grating is also a good way to stretch higher-fat cheese. While one ounce sliced doesn't seem like much, one ounce grated, or one-fourth cup, seems to go further.

If you want to go out, plan ahead about what you should and shouldn't order—then stick to your guns.

Where to find them:

- Great Greengrocers (national grocery chains specializing in organic foods)
- A&P
- Albertson's
- Dominica's Finer Foods
- Food Emporium
- Fred Meyer
- Grand Union
- Marsh Super Markets
- Public Super Markets
- Trader Joe's
- Winn-Dixie

Must Have Organic Convenience Foods

Organic foods have hit the Ice Age! Don't pass these meals by when you're strolling down the freezer aisle looking for fast yet healthy food!

- **Amy's Kitchen Country Vegetable Pot Pie.** Tender pastry stuffed with vegetables and creamy béchamel sauce. For info, call 707-578-7188.

- **Amy's Kitchen Pesto Pizza.** A light, crisp crust with a hint of olive oil, topped with broccoli and tomatoes. For info, call 707-578-7188.

- **Cascadian Farm Organic Veggie Quickstart Meal Starter.** An organic Hamburger Helper. Southwest skillet style with smoky chipotle sauce, this one is especially delicious. Add tofu, chicken, or seafood to the mix of grains. For info, call 800-624-4123.

Fantastic Foods Hot Cereal. Not-too-sweet cereal in a cup, packed with whole grains. Just add hot water. For info, call 707-778-7801.

Horizon Organic Lowfat Chocolate Milk. It's hard to believe something so chocolaty can still be lowfat and yet also deliver almost a third of calcium's daily value. For info, call 888-494-3020.

Lundberg Family Farms Quick Brown Rice. Easy to prepare! Side dish in flavors such as Roasted Garlic Pesto and Exotic Wild Rice & Mushroom. For info, call 530-882-4551.

Pacific Foods of Oregon Organic Vegetable Broth. Great for whipping up soups and sauces, cooking grains, and sautéing vegetables. For info, call 503-692-9666.

Shari's Organics Spicy French Green Lentil Soup. A fat-free, low-sodium canned soup with homemade taste. For info, call 734-426-0989.

Organic Websites. This is the Center for Science in the Public Interest. Go to this site for the scoop on controversial foods; this award winning site developed by the most dogged groups tops them all: www.cspinet.org.

5 a Day. Here the National Cancer Institute and the Produce for Better Health Foundation offers creative tips for eating five servings of fruits and vegetables a day; for example, potato slices topped with salsa,

Congratulations! You've kept it healthy all week! Plan a weekend outing with your grandkids!

The Lazy Way

pinto beans, and cheese instead of nachos. Go to www.dcpc.nci.nhi.gov/5aday.

- **Tufts University Nutrition Navigator.** Bypass search engines and go directly to the head of the class. The site's advisory board of nutrition experts rates more than 260 food websites—from pork producers to soy foods, Hershey's to Healthy Choice—for their content and usability. Just go to www.navigator.tufts.edu.

- **Mayo Clinic Health Oasis.** Go to the "Diet & Nutrition" section and click on "Virtual Cookbook" to have a dietician lighten up those old artery-clogging family recipes. Check it out at www.mayohealth.org.

Getting It Delivered!

Would you like someone to deliver fresh organic produce to your doorstep? You might consider joining your nearby Community Supported Agriculture Farm. Send a self-addressed, stamped envelope to Community Supported Agriculture Network (CSAN), Box 608, Belchertown, MA 01007, Attn: Michelle Wiggins, or visit the website at www.umass.edu/umext/CSA.

Here are some other folks who'd be happy to bring their garden to your house!

- **Door to Door Organics.** Those who live in eastern New York, Connecticut, New Jersey, Delaware, Maryland, Pennsylvania, and Virginia can have Door to Door Organics deliver a box of fresh produce

QUICK 🐭 PAINLESS

weekly. You pick the size, up to 36 pounds. For info, call 888-283-4443.

■ **Herban Kitchen.** This New York City restaurant and caterer offers organic dishes from its dinner menu Monday through Friday. For info, call 212 627-2257, or go to www.herban.com on the Internet.

■ **Straus Family Creamery.** Straus offers home delivery of BGH-free dairy products, including cream, milk, butter, yogurt, and cheese, in the San Francisco Bay area. For info, call 415-663-5464 or go to www.strausmilk.com.

■ **Urban Organic.** This Brooklyn-based service delivers organic produce weekly to residents of New York City's five boroughs of Westchester County, Long Island, and parts of Connecticut and New Jersey. For info, call 718-499-4321 or go to www.urbanorganic.com.

■ **Yoganics.** Yoganics delivers organic fruits, vegetables, and more than 100 grocery items to people living in Los Angeles and Orange county, California. For info, call 800-4yoganics.

YOU'LL THANK YOURSELF LATER

Congratulations! You're on the road to healthy eating. So go ahead and splurge. Enjoy a gourmet meal and eat anything you want once a week!

Getting Time on Your Side

	The Old Way	The Lazy Way
Making grilled veggies	20 minutes	2 minutes
Marinating foods	25 minutes	2 minutes
Making a complete meal	1 hour	5 minutes
Letting fast-food restaurants ruin your healthy diet	All the time	Never again!
Wondering what's really in the food you're eating	All the time	Never again!
Eating only salad when you go out	All the time	Never again!

Peace of Mind in 10 Minutes

Just because you've gotten wiser as you've gotten older doesn't mean your life is free from problems and stress, am I right? The time is now to review the importance of meditation and to learn, in only 10 minutes, how you can use it to experience each moment of your life with calm awareness.

GET THE FACTS!

I know, I know, you think about meditating or trying some of the other New Age stress-busters, but you "just don't have the time." Well, don't worry, because you're in very good company. Did you know that all the great masters of the meditative process wondered if they were meditating properly? They suggest that you don't try to suppress these thoughts, just surpass them. You have to let your conscious mind know that you are in charge by always returning to the meditation at hand.

Finding the Silver Lining

Sure, there are times when it is downright impossible to see the good in things gone wrong. After all, what positive things happened when your car broke down in the dead of winter, or your computer crashed as you were trying to meet a deadline?

The good news is that pessimism is just a habit, and it's one that can be broken! Here are some easy strategies to get rid of negative attitudes:

- Don't think the worst; weigh the evidence
- Don't blame yourself when things go wrong
- Keep a list of daily accomplishments and review it regularly
- Get enough sleep
- Eat balanced, nutritious meals
- Exercise regularly
- Act your way into right thinking

In with the Good—Out with the Bad!

Wait until I tell you another easy way to calm your mind and body. Breathing! Yes, it seems hard to believe, but breathing is a critical link between mind and body. Zen Buddhists use breathing as a focus for meditation; Taoists use it to help them connect with the energies of heaven and earth; and Jewish mystics rely on breathing exercises to help them unite with God.

No, you don't have to sign away all your worldly possessions and join a monastery to get the full effect of this important exercise. It's vital when learning how to

QUICK ⊂▥⊃ PAINLESS

Did you know that you can think and sleep your stress away, that the most energy you have to expend is to breathe? How easy can life get? First of all, if you can develop an optimistic outlook on life, you can really decrease your stress level.

meditate, and that's what this chapter is all about! Just follow the easy steps I've outlined to help you institute meditation in your daily life.

REWARD YOURSELF!

Some people feel that meditating is just a way to goof off or to waste time. This is not true, for you're doing something that, in the end, will reap mental, physical, and spiritual rewards far above what you would imagine. So I'm pleading with you to just take a leap of faith and indulge yourself in one of the oldest practices common to almost every culture on the planet. I promise you that once you start, you'll be as convinced as I am that your brain and body are inextricably intertwined.

Using What You've Already Got

Believe it or not, you're not learning anything new, because you'll actually be re-introducing yourself to skills and insights you didn't even know you possessed! Let this ancient practice give you back what time has taken away—and it takes only 10 minutes a day!

Thinking Yourself Fit

Detailed research reveals that meditation produces important cardiovascular, cortical, hormonal, and metabolic benefits, as well as significant beneficial alterations of interior experience, perception, and self-image. The physical benefits enhanced include the following:

- Boosts energy.
- Increases stamina.

YOU'LL THANK YOURSELF LATER

Because you're so busy during the day, why not get up earlier in the morning to meditate, or meditate before you go to sleep? That way you'll be able to concentrate more fully.

IF YOU'RE SO
INCLINED

Make your own meditation tape; that way you can control the time periods. Start it with the traditional three gongs (buy an inexpensive bell), ending your time with one gong!

- Lessens the severity and frequency of asthma attacks and allergic reactions.

- Lowers blood pressure.

- Reduces stress and stress-related illnesses, like heart disease, hypertension, and insomnia.

- Can dramatically reduce the incidence of the physical pain of arthritis, back injury, and most other causes. Of course, all of this is important to us to help reverse the aging process. Why cheat yourself when you can take full advantage of learning this important technique designed to eliminate the preceding infirmities!

GETTING THE HANG OF IT

There are four requirements to aid in producing a positive meditative state. Try hard to accomplish these four things prior to every meditation session. If you succeed, you'll be able to experience a much more satisfying meditation!

1. A quiet environment to reduce distractions

2. Comfortable posture providing complete relaxation

3. A few moments spent relaxing

4. Development of a mantra or prayer to help block the flow of conscious thoughts created by our waking state

Starting Off Right

Start on the road to clearing your mind by getting off on the right foot! If you clear your space, you'll have cleared your way to a good meditation at the same time! Here are a few tips to help you get there:

- Take the phone off the hook
- Take off your shoes
- Make sure there is nothing on the stove or in the microwave
- Make sure the TV or stereo is off

Jumping In—Feet First!

Meditating well means that you have to create a state of relaxed focus. No tense muscles need apply! Here's a routine you'll end up wondering how you ever lived without during your kid's terrible-twos stage!

1. Starting from your feet first, slowly relax all your muscles, ending with your neck, head, and face.

2. Breathe in and out slowly and naturally.

3. Close your eyes, but remain alert.

4. Tell yourself you would like to begin to remember certain life experiences that were extremely pleasurable and that you were so deeply involved in the activity that:

   - It seemed timeless; there was only the present moment.
   - You felt unmoved by past and future memories.
   - You were *being* instead of *doing*.
   - Your experiences can be visual (that sunset over the Bay of Acapulco) or auditory (that incredible performance by your favorite singer, the sound of a stream in the forest).

Congratulations! You've cleared your mind—and your house—of all distractions! The successful meditation you'll be able to have is the greatest reward!

The Lazy Way

Don't be a pessimist! Count even the smallest thing as an achievement. You might surprise yourself with just how much you really do every day!

5. Focus on that which asserts itself most predominantly. Now holding that memory in your mind, begin to examine it closely, minutely. Let that memory reverberate through your entire body. Can you sense the feeling of actually being in that moment now? Can you recall the timeless quality of just being in that moment?

6. Let yourself go now, and don't interfere with it. Don't read more into it than it is. Only experience the moment—and now you can open yourself to that moment with calm awareness.

7. As you end your session, stop and open your eyes. Pause to feel the experience of the body and mind.

Now is not the time to leap up and race around. Take a few minutes to do the following:

- Ask yourself: Do you feel any different? Good? Bad?

- Congratulate yourself! Even if you feel that you haven't accomplished anything before sitting down to do your meditation, you've actually achieved a very positive activity for the day after you were done!

- Arise and walk!

A BREATH OF FRESH AIR

Now we're getting to the really good part of this chapter. I'm going to give you a simple lesson in breathing. That's right, you may not be doing it right! Yikes! Maybe you are among the millions of people who take this autonomic bodily response for granted. Chances are you may never notice you're doing it wrong. So what's the point, you say? Well, if done right, it can help you conquer pain, avoid heart attacks, and even find peace and serenity in the midst of your day.

Finding a Healthy Rhythm

While the body takes care of the need for oxygen by making us breathe when we are not paying attention, like driving the car or watching television, we can voluntarily affect the rate, depth, and rhythm of our breathing whenever we choose. And in doing so, we can affect the subtle workings of not only our lungs, but also of our circulatory system, our organs, and every cell in our bodies.

When we can control our breath; we can also control our nervous systems and in turn our emotions and attitudes. In fact, recent research has shown that shallow, rapid breathing makes us feel chronically anxious, fatigued, and disoriented. Just as improper breathing can affect the mind and body in negative ways, healthy breathing can affect us in positive ways.

Breathing is really the critical link between the mind and body. This is a connection so strong that millions of people from all over the world have been using its techniques and methods to deepen their spiritual lives.

Most of us learned the basics of how the respiratory system works at some stage of our education process. We take in oxygen when we inhale and release carbon dioxide when we exhale. Yet despite this seemingly simple fact, most of us develop bad breathing habits. If you have poor posture, which collapses the upper body, your

IF YOU'RE SO
INCLINED

Have a camcorder at home? Set it up in the living room and let it watch you while you watch TV. Later, check out the tape and see how you're doing with your posture and breathing!

Make your inner and outer life your monastery. Wherever you are, whatever you come up against, you'll be able to approach that particular moment with serenity, with instant meditation.

breathing will be poor. Other people breathe from their chests, not their abdomens.

Breathe your way to better health with this simple routine:

1. Take a posture you can hold comfortably. Seated in this posture, take four deep, slow breaths. Notice that you are in control of your breath at this point.

2. Become aware of your breathing. No matter what you think of it, do not try to control it. Just be aware of it.

3. Continue to settle into your breath. At the same time, let go of it. Allow the breath to flow the way it wants to flow. Your breath knows what to do. It will, on its own, settle into its own pace.

4. Become aware of the gaps and pauses between exhalations and inhalations. These are called the **stillpoints**.

5. Become a natural observer of these stillpoints as the breath ebbs and flows, moving of its own accord. It's an endless sea of life. Sit like this for several minutes.

6. Watch your inhalation as the air flows in. Notice the moment of inhalation and exhalation. Watch the exhalation as the air exits.

7. Count each exhalation up to 10. Silently repeat one, one, one as you inhale and until your lungs are full. As you exhale, count two, two, two until you're finished exhaling.

8. Continue following this process until you have watched and continuously labeled four sets of consecutive inhalations/exhalations. Continue this process for your timed period of meditation. When you're done, gently open your eyes. Take this feeling of calm awareness with you for the rest of the day.

Don't be surprised if, in the middle of your meditation period, your thoughts go something like this: "Oh, my gosh. I'm meditating! Hey, I'm not thinking. Wait a minute; that was a thought! Darn it. Maybe I'm just flipping out! Where are those instructions? Wait a minute, my breath, I have to concentrate, get my breath back, okay, there it is. Maybe I just didn't start out right. Okay, I'm back."

BY GEORGE, I THINK YOU'VE GOT IT!

Once you've become more advanced in your meditative process, you can actually learn to meditate while you're doing such ordinary chores as washing dishes, peeling vegetables, sweeping the floors, taking out the garbage, and even scrubbing your bathroom down! Here are some strategies to help transform those various chores into something more meaningful:

- Do one thing at a time

- Concentrate on each movement required

- If your mind wanders, bring it back

Meditate Your Way Through Your Chores

Just do the physical act required without thinking about it. When you do the dishes, feel the water as it splashes

A COMPLETE WASTE OF TIME

The 3 Worst Ways to Treat Meditation:

1. To think that meditation is confined to your certain spot where you meditate.

2. To try to get high from the experience; it is merely a stage upon the way.

3. To try to rush it.

against your hands. Notice the appearance of the dish before and after you wash it. Taking out the trash, sweeping, dusting, and mopping should turn into "walking meditation."

Bernard Galssman says, "The cleaning process itself changes the cook as well as the surroundings and the people who come into those surroundings—whether we are in a Zen meditation hall, a living room, a kitchen, or an office."

Think about this! Any place can be a tranquil place for you if you will it to be! When you grocery shop, concentrate as you place each item into your cart as if you were building a rock garden.

Pay close attention to the food you eat. This action could be the very thing you need to practice when you're trying to lose weight. Notice the amount of food you are eating. Pay attention!

YOU DESERVE IT!

By now you've probably figured out that the practice of meditation can award you with a reprieve from your emotional life. Frustration, anger, stress, disappointments, and the like can disappear with the fine art of meditation. You'll begin to gain insight into the truth of who you really are. You will see that your perception is actually shaped by the various thoughts, ideas, and sensations that arise by themselves and pass by themselves. You can't control them, but it's no big deal!

Meditation will keep you from running around in circles and provide you a chance to center yourself. I now

Congratulations! You have added another tool to slow down the aging process: meditation. Now why don't you light some candles, burn some yummy incense, and take a nice warm bubble bath with your favorite music, flooding this space? Go ahead, you deserve it! Guess what? You may even feel yourself floating!

The Lazy Way

know why I love to do my "thang" on roller skates. It is truly my arena to embrace the meditative process. After five hours of this state, I'm still energized. Most people don't understand how I can do this for so long! Now you have some idea as to my secret. You, too, can find a similar path.

Freeing your mind to "float" without interference and control leads to an acceptance of what just *is*. Acceptance is the key to the amount of serenity you'll experience in your everyday life. This is the freedom that leads to true happiness.

QUICK 🔲 PAINLESS

When was the last time that you felt truly energized? What were you doing? Find a way to bring that energy into your every-day life! It's easy once you know where to start from!

Getting Time on Your Side

	The Old Way	The Lazy Way
Trying to "relax" during waking hours	3 hours	0 minutes
Therapy	45 minutes	10 minutes
Doubling your energy	30 minutes	30 seconds
Letting the little stuff get you down	All the time	Not anymore!
Listening to yourself	Never	Every day
Meditating for health	Never	Every day

Soulful Retreats

With all the knowledge and easy, practical applications you've learned up to this point, you're now ready to ascend to the next level! Believe it or not, that next step is to learn how to have your mind, body, and soul pampered by experts!

It's time to stop living as if you'll never have the time to pamper yourself just because you're busy. When we're at our busiest times is when we need to make that little extra effort to pamper ourselves the most. Learning how to create soulful retreats for yourself is a major part of keeping you together, calm, and ready for anything.

FINDING SOMEONE TO HELP YOU ON YOUR PATH

The meditation you've already learned about in Chapter 7 is going to be a large part of this. Finding a teacher, master, guide, spiritual guide, or "guru" is your first step to enhancing your meditative process. You're going to have many questions that need answers; therefore, you need to address this area if you're going to go on to deepen your experience in

There are three qualifications for a good teacher, so keep these in mind as you search for this person:

- **She contributes to your life; she doesn't control it.**

- **She is not in it for selfish motives, only to be gratified by your respect.**

- **She leads and guides in a loving, unselfish manner.**

being one with your universe. This is a must if you're on the "fast track" of life!

The "guru" relationship is not desirable if it does not require or create any independent thinking on your part. It can, however, be very beneficial if the guru's motives are spiritually aligned. Use your sixth sense to detect these differences.

Another kind of teacher is called a **Kalyana** or "spiritual friend." This is a very popular concept that's used in many religious and meditative traditions. This relationship consists of strong guidance and leading by example. She will ask questions and help lead, but definitely leaves the decision-making and follow-through up to you. Other traits for your spiritual friend would be:

- You are not subservient to your teacher.

- You do not put him or her in a position of power over you.

- Your teacher should be an experienced guide on your journey.

The Media Dimension

With all the demands on your time and life, some of the contemporary teachers of today have put out video tapes, audio tapes, and books that provide you with an instant jump start to more knowledge. This gives you an opportunity to connect instantly and obliterate the barriers of time and distance. I have created an audio tape and video that act as a "companion" piece to my system.

There is no substitute for the real thing, so look for my seminars and personal appearances throughout the year.

Now you're ready to contemplate a divine experience and go on your first meditative retreat! Yes, you can spend anywhere from three days to over a week in a setting to get your "head back" and get truly emotionally, spiritually, and physically centered!

I've observed that most people, when confronted with the opportunity to "get away from it all," immediately try to become anonymous in a sea of faces at a resort or other vacation spot. They never seem to get the idea that their mind, body, and spirit need to be treated to recharge their batteries for their return home. But you can make that change, because this book and chapter has made you more in tune with your rewards for doing so.

A meditation retreat is designed to provide you with the optimal setting for an intense experience of learning this practice.

Here are some of the quick 'n' painless activities of a retreat:

- Schedule and meals are made for you.
- Your actions yield clear, instant feedback; you instantly realize what you have done.
- You will spend time and be able to connect with a teacher involved in therapeutic sessions with your master teacher, as well as group meetings.
- You will experience a lessening of pain, anger, and suffering.

A COMPLETE WASTE OF TIME

The 3 Worst Things You Can Find in a Spiritual Group or Leader:

1. Meditation groups with the leader focusing on ethics and money—particularly if they are not practicing what they preach!

2. Groups that dress, groom, and act like their leader.

3. Members who do what they are told even if it violates their own code of ethics.

So now that you know what to expect, which will be the right one for you? The following is a list for you to consider when choosing:

- Nonreligious retreats are available.

- Zen centers will ask you to participate in religious service.

- Ask questions before you plunk down your hard-earned money in the form of a deposit!

- Your first retreat should not last any more than four days. Prepare to stay the full time of your commitment.

- You should be aware that various retreats have a variety of duration and intensities. Following are some suggestions to consider to make your choice more enjoyable.

Finding the Perfect Match

Make sure that you're selecting a retreat that suits you. Pick one that is within your means financially and one whose purpose and setting you're comfortable with. Now is not the time to try something completely foreign or to spend money you don't have. You need to be as comfortable as you can when embarking on a retreat like this!

Be aware that some have a "boot camp" type setting and may be too rigid for you, and make sure that the one you choose is one that you feel you can follow through with. Carefully consider what will be asked of you while participating in this retreat, and answer yourself

A COMPLETE WASTE OF TIME

The 3 Things Your "Soulful Retreat" Should Never Include:

1. This is not a vacation destination. This is not a party hearty "thang."

2. This is not the luxurious "spa" experience. It usually is simple and utilitarian.

3. You will not have a private room. Some monasteries are offering these prayer and meditation retreats.

honestly as to whether or not you can live up to their expectations as well as your own!

Be honest about what you need to be comfortable. Is their middle of nowhere location something that makes you nervous? You don't need to be marooned at the top of a snowy mountain to be able to experience an effective retreat! So make sure that you're happy with where you will be during the period of the retreat.

Once you have decided on a retreat experience and have actually booked one, you need to know exactly how to pack for one. Keep in mind that you cannot leave the grounds once you get there unless an emergency arises. You will most likely be miles from any major drugstore or department store, so plan accordingly.

Pack 'n' go:

- Meditation cushion and sitting mat
- Flashlight
- Thong sandals or slip-ons; you'll probably have to remove your shoes at the door of the meditation area
- Light blanket
- Your prescription medicines, soap, toiletries, and shampoo
- Notebook and pen
- Rain gear
- Cotton socks
- Winter wear—if weather requires
- Alarm clock

Bring your favorite perfume spray or body lotion, because the overall rule of thumb for meditative centers is to not wear, smell, or do anything to offend the process of your fellow meditators! If you are going to smell, smell pretty! But make sure that this is acceptable to the people who are running the retreat, as some request that no perfumes be worn.

While on your retreat, concentrate on not doing a few things that are detrimental to your process: talking, complaining, and schmoozing. If you avoid these pitfalls, you'll come to realize that most of these activities are meaningless and time wasters. As you get older, remember that time is valuable, and how you choose to spend it is crucial to your quality of life.

After a few days of silence, you might be so bored with your own inner dialogue that you find it necessary to communicate with someone else. Don't give in to that temptation because you're really just about to make a breakthrough. Hang in there! You're at the point when you are about to experience the most profound serenity you have ever felt.

What's It Going to Cost Me?

The costs of the retreat will be calculated for the facility and the number of days you attend. Part of the fees will be for your room and board. These fees range from 30 to 80 dollars per day. Some retreats also offer a scholarship for those who may be "financially challenged."

You'll also be expected to donate a small amount of money to your teacher(s), based on your ability to give.

A COMPLETE WASTE OF TIME

The 3 Worst Things You Can Do During a Retreat:

1. Talking to others; you'll interfere with the process.

2. Complaining.

3. Networking; there's a time and a place for schmoozing, and this isn't one of them!

The idea of a retreat is to be able to leave a monetary token as a "gift" for your experience you've received.

This "giving" is considered to be a necessary component to your experience because this opens up one's heart, allowing for the flow of agape love and denies the existence of greed and selfishness.

FINISH UP BY LOVING YOURSELF

Now that you've begun to dabble with the meditative side of life, it's time to spice it up a bit and learn to love yourself so much that you won't be looking for your loved ones to give it to you on demand. This part of the chapter will enhance your body, mind, and spirit and truly turn that clock back 15 to 20 years. We're going to talk about the ultimate spa experience and how you can benefit from it.

I used to be involved with La Costa Hotel and Spa in Carlsbad, California, and got to know how this elite spa operated, inside and out. Then I would travel to various spas throughout the world, to see which ones I liked and why. I even became hooked on the city of Acapulco and what was offered there.

Through these experiences, I learned how to unknot the knots, melt the tension, and find my "center." In these settings, relaxation and pampering rules. You decide which exercise class to take, what body treatments to indulge in, and what you want to eat. The job of every spa is to make you feel even better than when you came in.

IF YOU'RE SO
INCLINED

Most retreats have bulletin boards where you can post and receive certain messages. Just write and wait.

Whether your idea of heaven is to be involved in a beautiful spa and fitness facility offering instructor-supervised cardio and weight training classes, massage, beauty treatments, or simply to "chill" in a hammock or on a floating raft in a pool drenched by the sun, is up to you. Of course, you'll jump at the chance for all of this pampering—who wouldn't?

I hope that by rereading this system for turning back the clock *The Lazy Way,* you'll be inspired to take this chapter seriously and embark on completing your life, no matter what age you are, to optimal happiness and health! The brochures never tell you the lifelong friendships you make at these spas, nor the life-changing skills you'll learn to help you become healthy, fit, and stress free. They cannot describe the joy you feel when you tap into the incredible sense of empowerment you have attained as you apply this process of wellness as you approach your advanced years.

I'll also show you how you can create a space for yourself where you can just be; my description of a home spa–like setting will accomplish just that.

We're all capable of making our lives healthier, and armed with the information in this chapter, you'll surely succeed. The commitment and the first step are crucial, but you can do it. I know you can!

WHICH WAY DO I GO?

You might be lucky enough to know exactly where you want to go. Maybe you've kept this picture in your mind through the last 20 years of child rearing, working, and,

QUICK ✦ PAINLESS

Pampering can be as easy as taking the phone off the hook and enjoying a book, so don't overlook the easy way!

simply put, just being a '90s woman! Now you've finally decided to work on yourself. On the other hand, maybe your doctor recommended that you take a little R&R. You may be in a transitional period in your life, or you just may need a little variety.

YOU'LL THANK YOURSELF LATER

Read up on your destination and try to find out from friends about their experiences.

But maybe you're not too sure as to what you need from the spa experience. What the heck, part of the adventure is facing the unknown. All you need to know is that you want to return with a tension-free body, accentuated by glowing skin, and a body firmer and trimmer than ever. Most importantly, you want to learn how to maintain this forever. I personally would not recommend waiting 20 plus years.

How do you choose a spa? Do you want one whose focus is on spa activities only or a resort spa offering vacation options such as golf? My personal favorite, if you haven't guessed already, is a resort spa. If you're alone and want to focus on lifestyle changes, you might want to opt for the former.

Here are some options to keep in mind as you start your search:

- Choose whether you want a co-ed or women-only spa.
- A spa in the desert, mountains, forest, or by the ocean?
- Spartan, inexpensive, or high-priced—take your pick!

Okay, you've made your choice. What next? Well, book it! Now you have to rush like crazy to get everything

Leave your laptop and cell phone at home. Tell your office not to call. Take a journal because spas offer you an opportunity to tap into your creativity. Protect yourself from the heat; bring a sun hat and loads of sunscreen. These are definite age-erasers!

done before your trip. Packing, paying your bills, getting work done ahead of time, whew!

Open Your Mind

Be open to forming new relationships. Try sitting with a different group of people for meals.

Live in the moment. Indoors or outdoors, most spas are rich with color, texture, and smells. These are to be treasured, so enjoy!

Take risks! Try something you've never done before! Try a sport or activity you've never tried before. You may be pleasantly surprised by this new behavior and incorporate it into your life when you return home.

Don't forget to let the staff members help you; after all, that's their job! They have a definite system for indoctrinating you into their system of spa experiences. You'll probably start out with an orientation meeting, an individual meeting, and possibly an interview and checkup with the spa physician.

If you can possibly work out in the sports or activities you enjoyed before your trip, all the better. If not, don't become a spa warrior and try to make up for lost time. Moderation is the key. You'll need the proper balance to experience all the activities of the spa. Wave bye-bye to compulsive behavior.

On your return to reality, you may think you'll continue with your schedule, but don't delude yourself. Spas would not exist if this were so.

Instead, try to understand what made you experience such a fantastic way of life. Was it the quiet nook you created for yourself next to a running brook or gar-den? Was it that brisk walk before breakfast? How about that great massage and how relaxed it made you feel? Maybe you can make a commitment to yourself that you'll incorporate one or more of those changes you like the most into your daily routine.

Keeping It Going at Home

When you're getting "cabin fever," decide to take your-self to a day spa now and then. This will reinforce your spa experience as you flood your being with a state of bliss once again.

QUICK 🔲 PAINLESS

Want a great beauty break? Schedule one hour at a day spa and get a great massage. You can even opt for a 30-minute facial, body wrap, mud masque, herbal bath, salt glow, hydrotherapy treat-ment, or reflexology treat-ment.

Getting Time on Your Side

	The Old Way	The Lazy Way
Uncovering mystical places	1 day	1 minute
Building up your immune system	Weeks	5 minutes
Keeping yourself focused	Impossible!	Every day
Finding the right retreat for you	Where do I start?	I know exactly what I need!
Enjoying your retreat	Never	Every moment!
Mood control	Days	15 minutes

Quick Home Cures

We know today that people don't deteriorate and die just because they get older. Earthlings "kick" because they injure themselves or contract a disease. Even if you do not develop a major degenerative disease such as cancer, progressive oxidative damage to your brain—which controls everything else—can eventually get you. But not you, dear reader. I'm about to give you the solutions to conquering this process.

Hold on to your corsets, ladies; I'm going to enlighten you with the latest Fountain of Youth discovery. Just think, you only have to spend two seconds to get the results. Hogwash, you say? Listen up! There have been all kinds of research on nutritional supplements to help stave off the aging process and at the same time provide you with buffers to hinder the onslaught of cancer, stroke, and heart disease.

SHED THOSE YEARS

Although most of you know the common-sense strategies to avoid degeneration and disease, I'll be offering you some

QUICK ⊕ PAINLESS

different strategies. Included will be things to extend your vital life by many years that you can start on immediately. Here's a list of tips to help you succeed in this area:

- Boost immunity
- Exercise daily
- Feed your brain with proper nutrients and supplementation
- Avoid negative triggers from people, places, and things
- Develop a trust in a power greater than yourself
- Eat less
- Above all, enjoy yourself—have a blast!

SUPPLEMENT YOUR HEALTH

Let's take a look into how you can boost your immunity through proper supplementation. Supplements can make a tremendous difference in how well your body can ward off diseases such as cancer, stroke, and heart disease. Some research states that the sooner you start, the more likely you'll be to not only cut the percentage of risk to 50 percent, but also to greatly improve your health and energy and even reverse severe health problems. Introducing the right supplements to your nutritional regime can make the difference between an active, healthy long life and crippling illness—even death.

Keep in mind that supplements and their benefits can be achieved only by combining them with a healthy lifestyle. Along with the need for supplements comes the need to exercise regularly, eat a nutrient-dense, low-fat diet, and maintain healthful habits.

Supplements can work in a variety of ways. There are those that can protect against cell damage—which is the basis for many types of cancer and heart disease—called **antioxidants**. There are others that are the building blocks for enzymes and hormones that help the body recover and protect itself.

GIVE YOURSELF A HORMONE BOOST

Let's get to the most dramatic supplement first. Dehydroepiandrosterone (DHEA) is a hormone that declines rapidly in our body as we get older. Supplementation has shown that one can reverse those ravages visited upon the graying of America.

The most recent example of DHEA's benefits is a study that shows men with the highest DHEA levels have better cardiovascular health. In addition, they also have leaner, younger looking bodies, with low body fat. DHEA has also been rumored to combat certain kinds of arthritis. Are you ready for this next statement? DHEA has shown in many cases to improve brain functioning and reduce depression, and boost your immunity! Take as directed.

Testosterone vs. Viagra

There are cutting-edge clinics in Europe that are trying to help men age 40 to 60 and higher fight male menopause (viripause) with the male hormone testosterone. They are trying to get these men to fight the aging process and restore their virility.

YOU'LL THANK YOURSELF LATER

Avoid foods and other products that contain aluminum, which has been associated with Alzheimer's disease. These include many processed foods, antacids, antiperspirants, and even some toothpastes.

Viagra addresses only male potency, while testosterone has been known to increase muscle mass, strength, and lower body fat. Recent findings have targeted the aging process for men to directly affect their body's natural decline in testosterone. This has a dramatic affect on the aging male population.

But is the re-introduction of testosterone safe? Because anabolic steroids have been classified as controlled substances and narcotics, I don't think this is the proper way to go. These therapies tend to cause more problems than they are worth. With that in mind, is there another solution? Men, or you ladies involved with men whose advancing years are freaking them out, have no fear! There are safe solutions.

Turbo-Charge Your Brain

To combat the decline of memory, one needs to take the following:

- **Pycnogenol.** An antioxidant that protects brain cells from damage related to stress and pollution.

- **L-Carnitine.** This amino acid helps the brain produce neurotransmitters. This helps reduce age-related memory decline and in some cases prevent Alzheimer's.

- **Ginseng.** This herb helps the brain and body withstand stresses of all kinds and can improve memory.

- **Pregnelone.** This is a hormone that decreases with age. By taking Pregnelone, you can improve your memory and enhance learning skills.

- **CoQ10.** This helps to oxygenate the brain and can

improve symptoms of Alzheimer's.

- **Ginko bilboa.** This improves blood circulation in the brain and can improve memory.

- **Grapeseed extract.** Another antioxidant, this protects the brain and nervous tissue from damage.

- **DHEA.** This is one of the most all-inclusive supplements for preventing the aging process.

  Here are some more things to consider:

- **Antioxidant vitamins: A, C, and E.** These vitamins help protect the brain against damaging free radicals that have been associated with brain cell loss and Alzheimer's. Sometimes you can find them combined in one capsule. A daily dose would be 5,000 IU of A, 200 IU of E, and 500 mg of C.

- **Vitamin B-Complex with folic acid.** B vitamins are essential for anyone with memory problems. Low levels can contribute to distortion and memory problems. Take a 50 mg tablet twice a day.

- **Minerals.** Calcium, magnesium, potassium, copper, zinc, iron, and boron are all generally recognized as critical to brain function.

- **Lecithin.** This nutrient is used by the brain to produce a crucial neurotransmitter called **acetycholine.** It can boost brain function and memory in the elderly. Take a 1,200 mg capsule once or twice a day.

YOU'LL THANK YOURSELF LATER

Those of you who are already taking medications need to check with your physician before starting out on my system of supplementation.

The 3 Worst Things You
Can Do as Time Goes By:

1. Abusing alcohol: a
   leading cause of
   dementia.

2. Becoming a couch
   potato.

3. Eating a high-fat
   diet, with very little
   fruits and vegetables
   included.

A GUIDE FOR BEING A LONG LIVER

Cut your risk for cancer, stroke, and heart disease in half with vitamins, minerals, and herbs! Yes, you can complete your supplementation for anti-aging with this formula. What amount of time do you need to gulp a few supplements? Five minutes. That's all!! How easy can life get—especially when you don't have the time to check out all the volumes of information on this subject. Just take this list to your doctor, get his or her approval, and off you go!

The right supplementation program can make the difference between an active, healthy long life and crippling illness or even death.

I'll give you your shopping list of must-haves to keep you young, active, healthy, and vibrant! This has been compiled by various experts for preventing cancer, heart disease, and stroke.

- Vitamins

  - **Beta Carotine (Vitamin A).** This decreases the cell damage that leads to cancer and the buildup of cholesterol in blood vessels. Studies show that it reduces the risk of a variety of cancers, including lung cancer and oral cancer. Prescribed dosages are 10,000 to 15,000 IU.

  - **Vitamin C.** This reduces the risk of cancer and heart disease. For years scientists have known that this vitamin protects against chromosome damage that can lead to cancer. Studies have shown that it reduces the risk of various cancers. Take 1,000 mg every day in divided doses.

- **Vitamin E.** This reduces the risk of cancer, heart disease, and stroke. It also is key to reducing other kinds of cancer of the mouth, throat, neck, lungs, stomach, intestine, and colon. Other studies show it slows the development of coronary disease. Take 400 to 800 IU every day.

- **Folic acid.** This has been shown to reduce the risk of cervical and colon cancer.

- Secret mineral remedies

  - **Chromium picolinate.** This decreases the risk of heart disease and stroke by boosting the "good" HDL cholesterol. Take 600 micrograms daily.

  - **Selenium.** This reduces the risk of cancer, heart disease, and stroke. Studies reveal women who consumed the most had the lowest risks of breast cancer. It lowers the risk of stomach and lung cancer. Take 50 micrograms a day.

  - **Calcium.** This has been shown to lower blood pressure and is a preventative for colon cancer and heart disease.

  - **Magnesium.** This reduces the risk of stroke; it should be taken with calcium to maintain mineral balance. Take 250 mg twice a day. Some studies show it reduces blood pressure.

  - **Potassium.** This protects against high blood pressure and helps insure a regular heart beat. Take one 100 mg tablet per day.

YOU'LL THANK YOURSELF LATER

Pursue new hobbies and other interests, read, watch TV, go to movies, work the crossword puzzle, and go to school. Some research indicates that video games improve mental acuity in the elderly.

Congratulations! You've added helpful herbs to your diet. Treat yourself to some fresh flowers to boost your smile now that you've boosted your energy!

The Lazy Way

- Herbal wish list
  - **Green tea or green tea extract.** This helps to reduce cell damage and prevents certain cancers. It also keeps cholesterol from clogging arteries.
  - **Garlic.** This reduces the risk of cancer, heart disease, and stroke. Also shown to lower cholesterol.
  - **Hawthorn.** This reduces the risk of heart disease and stroke by helping provide energy to cardiac muscle cells.
  - **L-carnitine.** This cuts the risk of heart disease and stroke by helping provide heart cells with energy.

SLEEP

If sleep is a necessary ingredient in keeping your immune system in check, what do you do as you get older and you feel you may be experiencing a sleep disorder? Research shows that as you get older, your body does not require as much sleep. Some people complain of not getting enough sleep. Well, there is a solution!

Melatonin is a great supplement taken shortly before bedtime and correlates with the onset of rising melatonin levels in the body. Melatonin is absorbed rapidly and the most fast-release melatonin preparations help people fall asleep in 30 minutes.

As with any other medicine or supplement, check with your doctor first before you start using melatonin.

LADIES CHOICE

Ladies, are you listening to me? Spend one minute reading this, and you'll find a quick fix to your menopausal distress. Menopause is a natural progression—transition from one life to another. The secret is to help ease you into this phase as naturally and gently as possible. Hot flashes? Weight gain? Depressed? Low energy? Anxious? No more, and you don't have to run to your doctor for your latest hormonal prescription.

First of all, the low-fat, high-protein diet mentioned in this book will help balance your body's hormones and help you regulate your sexual hormone production. This is critical when you need to keep your sugar stable. Level blood sugar helps prevent hot flashes, depression, and mood swings, while helping you to lose weight effortlessly. With this food program, you need the right supplements to help zap this problem area you're faced with or will be faced with!

For your shelf:

- **Flaxseed oil** to use in your cooking.
- **Evening primrose oil** converts into hormones like prostaglandins.
- **M&M's**—no, not the candy—is a multivitamin and magnesium combination that gets your hormonal system back into balance.
- **Zinc** lowers estrogen and increase progesterone levels.
- **Natural progesterone cream.**
- **Exercise** 30 minutes, five days a week, or housercise!

YOU'LL THANK YOURSELF LATER

It just takes a few minutes to swap in healthy items to your cabinets. So, what are you waiting for!

■ **Soy Phyoestrogens** are soybeans and certain other plants rich in mild plant estrogen that can occupy your cell estrogen receptors and reduce the undesirable effects of estrogen. They can help balance fluctuating hormone levels.

All of these items can be found in your local health food store as tablet, tinctures, creams, or sublingual drops.

■ Black Cohash

■ Dong Quai

■ Raspberry leaves

■ Chasteberry (vitex)

■ Wild Yam

■ Rehmannia

■ Licorice Root

The pollution, pesticides, packaging of foods, and processing methods eliminate many of the vitamins and minerals needed to maintain a healthy body. That's why this chapter is so important to study, study, and study again. Once you've digested this material, you'll be on your way to maintaining and improving your health! It would stand to reason that taking one of my suggestions for developing a quality of life would accomplish your purpose, but if you follow all of them, wow, what a life!

I usually take about 50 supplements a day and exercise seven days a week. I combine recreational activities and weight training to stay in top shape, but I'm an extremist and don't expect you to follow suit. But then

Congratulations! You have waded through the maze of supplementation and come to understand it all! Now take a break and treat yourself to a cup of coffee. Did you know that it stimulates dopamine production? (The "feel good" hormone.)

The Lazy Way

again, why not? If you're going to do something, why not give it your best shot? I am mentally alert, have tons of energy, and never get sick!

QUICK ⬤ PAINLESS

You deserve the best, right? Right! Well, take a few seconds every morning to remind yourself of that. It'll get you off on the right foot!

Getting Time on Your Side

	The Old Way	The Lazy Way
Brain boosting	Months	15 minutes
Hormonal treatments	Months	3 minutes
Understanding supplements	Help!	15 minutes
Knowing which foods to avoid and why	Help!	15 minutes
Learning how to sleep better	Impossible!	10 minutes
Sparking up your sex drive	Months	4 minutes

Chapter ten

Get a Hitch in Your Gidalong!

I **truly believe that the "Fountain of Youth" can be determined by your cardio-respiratory condition. Your overall physical and mental health is most affected by the health of your cardio-respiratory system. So how can you separate the mind and body? Do you want to live for 120 years?**

Be honest, most of us would not want to live past the time when we're no longer able to have a quality of life we can enjoy. So we've set up a catch-22 situation for ourselves, haven't we? We want to live out our lives 20 years longer than we thought we would, with all the advanced medical technologies, but we don't know if we can maintain our bodily health if studies show that aging is a degenerative disease. Here's the big question: how can we really have fun if we're facing a five day a week, 20-minute aerobic fitness program— yikes!—when we barely have enough time to fit an extra five minutes in our day?

Forget about growing old gracefully, we're interested in *not* getting old! By preventing and reversing degenerative conditions associated with aging—heart attack, atherosclerosis, diabetes, cancer, and so on—your "golden" years can be very vigorous and fulfilling.

Through my own experience and that of those who have gone before me, I can attest to the fact that what you can do in your early adulthood, you can do at 50, 60, 70, or 80, but you have to work at it. I know, when I tell my patients, this is when they put their hands over their ears. Then I tell them, "Hey, everyone wants to go to heaven, but nobody wants to die!" They usually settle down after that, because I'm standing in front of them and am usually older than all of them. They see the shape I'm in, and they get truly motivated, just as you can. You don't have to be an extremist like I am, but you do have to get focused and have the knowledge of what your body needs.

KEEP IT FUN!

Before we go a step further, I want to emphasize that your aerobic conditioning program should be fun! It should provide social, recreational components. And, yes, it should be emotionally gratifying as well.

The people who come to see me at my clinic and who have the best results are those who have discovered a special sport they enjoy. I can never stress this enough. They use their sport as a form of self-expression and emotional release and are gratified by the results. They rarely get bored and look forward to their aerobic activity with excitement.

Believe it or not, most people I've worked with thought that exercise + sport = jogging. Few got very excited about that. They hadn't thought of all the other ways they could strengthen and tone their lungs. As we explored their preferences regarding aerobic conditioning, they had discovered activities years ago that they could still be enjoying now. I also fill them in on new and exciting activities they could enjoy, and they're flabbergasted to know there is such a plethora of choices.

Each sport has its benefits and drawbacks. So I've taken the time to make you aware of them as we go through this chapter. If you're a beginner in any of the activities listed, you don't want to jump right into the advanced level. Swallow your pride and sign up for the novice or beginner classes or activities. Don't worry, you'll still get a good workout, and you'll be participating at your own level. If your arms and legs feel like lead, slow down, catch your breath, and then try to pick up the pace again. One sure way to really check out an activity you may have always wanted to try out is to purchase a video on the activity you're going to learn.

GETTING TO THE HEART OF THE MATTER

Aerobic exercise gets your heart pumping near its maximum capacity for an extended period of time. The exercises that are aerobic are those that use the large muscle groups in your arms and legs continuously. Walking, running, biking, and swimming are aerobic; and they give the most aerobic benefits when they're performed without stopping for 20 minutes. In these activities, your cardio-respiratory systems transport blood and oxygen to your muscles while removing lactic acid and carbon dioxide.

YOU'LL THANK YOURSELF LATER

To be comfortable and injury free is your main goal when you settle into your activity. The pace you set for yourself can either make the experience enjoyable and challenging or turn it into 60 minutes of agony. So make sure you're fully prepared for your choice, from your mindset to the shoes you put on, and you'll reap great rewards!

Anaerobic exercise is exercise that's performed in short bursts, rather than long periods. Weight lifting, sprinting, and sports such as tennis and racquetball get your heart pounding hard but provide breaks every few minutes, which allow the heart to slow down. Since they do not keep the heart rate up for an extended period of time, they are called anaerobic.

Outfit Yourself Right

Here are a few tips to get you through your first aerobic fitness day:

- Wear comfortable clothes
- Bring a water bottle—the bigger the better
- Bring a towel
- Sneak in a walk whenever you can; climb stairs instead of taking the elevator, or take a 15-minute walk on your lunch break
- Get an exercise buddy or join a club that sponsors one of your favorite activities
- Don't overdo it!

Hearty Helpers

Okay, you have the right clothing, and you're ready to go. But wait! Before you stride your way to youth, may I make a few suggestions?

You won't get sore if you start your program slowly. Follow the warm-up exercises outlined in Chapter 5 so you can allow your muscles to stretch and come alive slowly. Then you can work harder without causing pain.

QUICK ⬤ PAINLESS

Fidget frequently. Research has shown that "spontaneous physical activity" like tapping toes and fussing with hands blasts off up to 800 extra calories a day!

When you start, remember your muscles have probably been inactive for a long time. They need at least 24 hours after each workout. I recommend three times a week at first, with a full day off in between each session.

After two or three months, you can boost your workout schedule to four days a week, using a combination of days that fits your personal schedule and alternates exercise and resting days.

If you've been inactive for many years, here are some things you should do differently:

- Get a thorough physical exam by your doctor.

- Spend more time warming up and cooling down.

- Joint fluid diminishes with age, so skip anything requiring a tremendous amount of pressure on the joints.

- Pay more attention to your diet, eating more fruits and vegetables and much less fat.

Show Me How!

Let's take a look at some of the classes that might be offered at your local Y and or health club. Adult night classes are great, too!

- **Aerobics.** Designed to improve the cardiovascular system, tone the body, and reduce body fat, these classes contain a warm-up, 30-minute aerobic workout, muscle specific exercises, and then a cool-down and stretch. Different skill levels are offered, as well as low-impact sessions where you keep one foot on the ground at all times, taking pressure off the joints.

IF YOU'RE SO
INCLINED

Weight training can actually help prevent osteoporosis. And women, you will not get muscles. What you get is a beautiful body—fit and toned.

YOU'LL THANK YOURSELF LATER

Consider hiring yourself a personal trainer to teach you about weight training. Prices range from $25 to $125 an hour. More about that later.

Step aerobics. This is very similar to regular aerobics but uses a platform that you can raise to increase intensity.

Aquabics. As you might guess, this exercise is performed in the pool, where you feel totally weightless. This is an excellent option for people with joint and weight problems.

Spinning. Believe it or not, this is the latest craze! It's performed on a stationary bicycle. You'll sweat like crazy, but you can go at your own pace.

Hip-Hop. This is one of my favorites! If you like funky music, take this high-energy dance class. The moves are pretty intricate, so be forewarned.

Boxercise. Here's another hot sport that might make you feel like a boxing immortal—really! You'll learn techniques unique to boxing as you work off that donut you ate this morning. You'll definitely work out your arms and shoulders. Ladies, are you listening? You want to get rid of the upper arm flab, don't you?

Kardio kickboxing. All you have to do is throw kicks into the mix of upper cuts and jabs—simple, right? Don't be deceived, this is a great workout!

Body pump. This combines light weights with an aerobic workout. If you have never been exposed to weight training before, this is a good place to start.

Body sculpting. This is an aerobic workout where you use your body as the resistance factor. You can also use light dumbbells, rubber bands, stability balls, and weight bars.

ONE FOOT AT A TIME

For those who are considered truly beginners, I think you should start out with a walking program. It helps build stamina and endurance, improves circulation, and helps get your legs in shape. Walking helps you reduce anxiety and tension and burns body fat.

All the people I work with begin an aerobic walking program and find it easy to fit into their hectic schedules. As they advance, they do a walk-jog program. Here's your "Leave Youth in the Dust" walk/run cardio-respiratory exercise prescription:

- **Week One.** Once a day, three days per week, walk a distance of one-half mile in 10 minutes. You'll be walking at a rate of about three miles per hour.

- **Week Two.** Once a day, three days per week, walk a distance of one mile in 20 minutes.

- **Week Three.** Once a day, three days per week, walk a distance of 1½ miles in 30 minutes.

- **Week Four.** Once a day, three days per week, jog one-quarter mile.

STEPPING UP THE PACE

Once you begin running, you'll probably notice that you have a distinct running style. To maximize your benefits, learn to run with a heel first action and push off on the ball of your foot with each stride. Let your arms relax and curl your fingers into loose fists to help your running motion. Keep your body straight and relaxed. Start with short strides, lengthening as you progress. Breathe rhythmically and never hold your breath as you run!

QUICK PAINLESS

Make out madly! Even kissing kills calories. When you make out, put your whole body into it. The more you move, the more fat you'll burn.

MORE GREAT IDEAS!

You've seen the value of putting one foot in front of the other and just striding forward, but now think about adding a few things into your motion!

- **Cycling.** This gives you a great cardiovascular workout and is easy on the joints. If you're overweight, this is an ideal activity. Another benefit is getting in touch with your "inner child" and the sense of fun this activity provides. Another age eraser!

- **In-line and roller skating.** Of course, you know I had to mention this! This is my favorite activity! It meets every need I have in life and for my health. The health and cardiovascular benefits are outstanding! It tones your butt and streamlines your legs. And boy, does it burn fat! Take lessons first, please.

- **Swimming.** The rhythmic, powerful movements and sensual pleasures of swimming quickly release your mind from the tedious details of life, and you'll find yourself floating in a world of tranquillity and relaxation—what could be better?

- **Rowing and canoeing.** If you're a conditioned athlete, this is for you. If not, think of this activity as an alternative for you to choose as you get yourself in better shape. Rowing requires good back strength.

- **Hiking.** Hiking is great for getting outdoors and enjoying nature. Through the sheer enjoyment this activity provides, you can face obstacles that will test your physical agility. Hiking has become an increasingly popular sport, and it is one I recommend highly.

QUICK PAINLESS

You can run anywhere, anytime, as long as you take a few precautions for weather and safety. Just lace up your shoes and move on out!

- **Tennis.** Tennis is one of my favorite sports, and I used to teach it at John Gardiner's Tennis Ranch in Carmel Valley, California. I've played this sport for many years and love the overall body conditioning it produces. You can play tennis anywhere in the world as long as you have decent weather.

- **Golf.** This is another favorite of mine. Golf is excellent for developing eye-hand coordination but lousy for conditioning. Sure, you walk a lot, but most people I know take golf carts. Still, I enjoy playing this game, particularly in beautiful surroundings.

Some other activities I recommend you to consider are:

- **Yoga.** This is the latest craze—even Madonna swears by this. It's a series designed to improve flexibility and strength and to perfect breathing techniques. It's also a great stress buster!

- **T'ai Chi.** This is an ancient form of Chinese stress management and the perfect antidote to all the tension in your life.

TYING IT ALL TOGETHER

These recreational sports are but one aspect of your total fitness program. Most have cardiovascular and strengthening benefits, but to maximize these benefits, particularly if you are interested in toning and shaping your body, you should combine your sport with a weight-training program such as weight lifting.

YOU'LL THANK YOURSELF LATER

Give your man/woman a massage! Not only does an hour-long massage burn 230 calories, if it leads to what I think it will—an extra hour or so of passionate playtime—tack on another 270 calories killed. That's a total of 500 calories! Not a bad few hours investment if you ask me!

You need to be in shape to enjoy the sport you choose. The longer you play, the greater the cardio-respiratory benefits. The more often you participate in the sport you enjoy the most, the faster you'll improve your conditioning program.

If you have home access to aerobic machines such as a stair-climber, lifecycle, or treadmill, you're really ahead of the game! You can do your 20-minute cardio session at home!

BRINGING IN SOMEONE TO GET YOUR GROOVE ON

All right, back to hiring a trainer. They are good—pro-viding you get a qualified one—because they can teach you the subtleties of using weights and other exercise equipment. They can teach you how to grip a barbell, use cables and ropes, and how to adjust a machine for your strength requirements. If you answer yes to at least one of the following items, I suggest you hire a trainer.

Here's a quick quiz for you:

- Are you completely out of shape?
- Do you want to update your program?
- Do you need to reach a fitness goal but don't know how?
- Do you feel that you need someone to motivate you?
- Do you need to "rehab" an injury you're recovering from or have you recently undergone surgery for a problem joint?

Include your sports activity in your weekly schedule and treat it as you would any other important appointment. Schedule it in place of other workouts, three times a week, in writing. If you don't, obstacles and other priorities will invariably arise to push aside your fitness program. Schedule your playtime and take charge of your health and lifestyle.

Getting Time on Your Side

	The Old Way	The Lazy Way
Staying fit on the road	3 hours	20 minutes
Keeping fit	2 hours	0 minutes
Hiring an aerobic instructor	1 hour	20 minutes
Packing for your trip	Hours	20 minutes
Enjoying your workout	Never	Every second!
Taking care of yourself	I'll start tomorrow!	Every day!

eleven

Cruise Your Way to Health – Ageless Travel Tips

Back in Chapter 8, "Soulful Retreats," I told you about the various places you could go to get your head together. That chapter, however, was geared to exclude all stimuli from your environment. Now I'm going to take you in the opposite direction. Assuming you've worked through your mental cobwebs, you're now ready to balance that by pulling out all the stops when it comes to creating adventure in your life!

Everyone ascending the ladder of advancing age will experience some loss of excitement or adventure to their life. This is the necessary ingredient you need now to accelerate your adrenal glands, which in turn gives you a certain "joie de vive" attitude about life. The infusion of adrenaline also gives you a heightened sense of awareness of the joy of being alive!

If you are truly stuck in a hotel or motel that doesn't have anything, let your fingers do the walking! Check out the local health clubs. Treat your search as an adventure! Think about going to the local high schools or Ys to see if you can get a 45-minute workout in their weight room.

Assuming you've followed this book and applied each chapter as presented to your life, you're now ready to experience the panoply of opportunities to expand your world, life experience, and originality in your approach to developing a healthy lifestyle. This will greatly increase your longevity and at the same time provide you with a wonderful quality of life.

HOW TO KEEP AT IT—EVEN ON THE ROAD!

Consider this, you've jumped in feet first with my system to stop the aging process, and then your boss decides to ship you to Nebraska for a convention. "How will I be able to continue this if I have to go on a business trip or just go on vacation for a couple of weeks?" you ask yourself. Have no fear! There is a solution.

Nowadays, the easiest places for you to stick to your program are at hotels, airports, and other places you thought it would be impossible to continue with your health and wellness goals. Leaving town does not mean the annihilation of a successful application of your health and fitness regime! This chapter offers healthy alternatives to stick with your goals—even when you have to go "on the road" for business or vacation.

Making the Best of Your Hotel in Their Gym

When I was a flight attendant traveling all over the world—ahem, many years ago—finding a hotel with a full health club was rare. They usually had one stationary bike, one of those machines that jiggled your cellulite away (so they claimed), and a thigh and hip roller designed to do the same. If you could find a set of barbells, you were lucky!

Nowadays, it's a different story! The world has become so transient now that global travel is so affordable, accelerated by the increased need for the economic opportunities this affords. Therefore, to be competitive, hotels and resorts must provide their guests with the amenities they enjoy.

I swear, some hotels can rival health clubs for what they offer. One particular favorite of mine is the Mariott hotel in Palm Springs. This place has everything, including a spa and disco! I love going there! They also have high-tech machinery and free weights. Never mind their staff of on-call trainers, should you need one. There are television sets rigged from above so you don't get bored and headphones are provided for you at the treadmills, Stairmasters, and lifecycles if you want to listen to music! The Mariott, yes, is a "high-end" hotel. But there are many less expensive hotels that are equipped similarly.

Some hotel gyms are free to paying guests while others share a small fee. Here in New York, some hotels charge a fee of $25 a visit. Some hotels let you use their pool at no cost but will charge to use the other facilities. You almost always have to sign a waiver in case you injure yourself on the premises in any way. Basically, they're protecting themselves, and you proceed at your own risk.

Some hotels have even gotten so creative as to create rooms equipped with a bike, rowing machine, step

YOU'LL THANK YOURSELF LATER

Talk to your travel agent to find out which hotels have gyms and mini-spas. He or she usually has an updated list. Ask how much the gym costs and if it's on the premises, when it's open, and when it closes.

IF YOU'RE SO INCLINED

Another service you can ask for is to have equipment delivered to your room. This is not an uncommon practice for the famous people I've worked with who need to watch their body, mind, and spirit at all times. I can hear it now, "Room service, I'd like to have a tuna sandwich, hold the mayo, and one Stairmaster!"

machine, and exercise videos. Hotels here in New York have made arrangements with The Gym Source, an equipment dealer. All the guest has to do is order a piece of equipment like a treadmill or a multi-purpose weight machine, and it's sent to their room. Arnold Schwarzenegger and Sylvester Stallone are famous for doing this! When these two mega stars are on location, they've been known to order a mini-gym as part of the stipulations in their movie contract. (And you thought they looked that way naturally!)

Turning the Tables in Your Favor—The Options Are Endless!

If you're determined—like I have been—you can find a place to work out anywhere in the world. I have even been known to do some of my standing stretches and lunges in the subways of New York while waiting for a train! Having traveled all over the world most of my life, I know what I'm talking about! The greatest bodybuilder of all time, Dorian Yates, from Australia, built a gym in his basement and affectionately calls it the "Dungeon." He made his own equipment! Does this tell you something?

As a former physical education teacher, I know that you can always find alternative gym spaces. In the process, you'll get to know some really nice people and contribute to your anti-aging program by associating with those younger than you and experiencing the thrill of a new experience. You'll also be able to increase your awareness of other cultures as every town has its own uniqueness. You don't necessarily have to travel to Europe to get that experience.

One of the great things about sticking to your fitness program—which hopefully includes some weight training—is that you'll be able to take it on the road! (See, there is a method to my madness in teaching you the definitive ways to turn back the clock!)

Taking It Outside

My hometown is Carmel, California. Whenever I went to visit my parents, with my children in tow, I reveled in the natural beauty of this town. I would take my kids for long walks, along with my parents, and we loved seeing the creeks, horses, and other beautiful sights one would not ordinarily see if you didn't participate in this form of exercise. So don't cop out on me now. Remember, I treat walking as a form of aerobic conditioning. Good!

I usually stay in a bed-and-breakfast in the Marina District when I go to San Francisco, California. This spot is right near the Marina Greens—a favorite spot used by the locals for running and kite flying. It even has a par-course, where there are different exercise stations to take you on a complete workout. There are instructions on each station. As long as you can read, you don't even need a trainer! This kind of activity can really turn into your own outdoor health club, and it won't even cost you a dime!

If you can't satisfy your recreational interests with what they offer, you can always "let your fingers do the walking" one more time. The local Yellow Pages will

QUICK ⬤ PAINLESS

If you travel a lot, it might be a good idea for you to purchase a list of local gyms from the American Business Directory (it comes in disc format, too). This source has thousands of entries compiled from the Yellow Pages. If you go to Pocatello, Idaho, this list not only provides you with the name of the health club, but the address and phone number, too!

Most hotels have maps available at the concierge desk. They could even provide you with detailed maps of all the jogging and biking paths. If you ask them, they can illuminate your fitness excursion in the great outdoors with info on the most scenic routes. Some hotels will even provide you with fitness walking tours.

have a list of various associations, such as biking, running, skating, or other activities you can enjoy. Give them a call.

PACK YOUR BAGS!

If none of the previously mentioned plans is available, bring your own "traveling gym." Do you think I've taken leave of my senses? Not to worry. I always pack my own gym no matter what; and yes, you guessed it, I bring my roller skates! I've listed the following items to include in your "Bag of Tricks Traveling Gym":

- In-line skates
- Jump rope
- Foam step for your step workout (that way you won't break your back lugging it)
- Resistance rubber exercise bands
- Your favorite CDs, tapes, and walkman
- Exercise tape (dance, step, or low-impact)
- Small exercise mat (what you use for your meditation)
- Sneakers
- Water bottle

I agree, this may not be a stunning situation for you, but it will help you to stay consistent with your fitness program. It's all in the planning, and then you get to use that plan.

You can also use the hotel furniture to help you do sit-ups and abdominal crunches.

EATING ON THE RUN

A big thorn in my side when it comes to travel—sparked by a determination to stick to my eating habits—is airplane food. I used to be a flight attendant and am pleased to announce that after years of research, I discovered some fascinating bits (excuse the expression) of information. The good news is the airlines have cleaned up their act! Many airlines will allow you to order a special meal along with your ticket.

What happens if you forget to order your meal? This has happened to me. I usually take my own lunch box consisting of bottled water, fresh fruit, grilled chicken or turkey, and whole grain crackers, and voila!—instant perfect meal!

If you happen to be detained by an airport layover, you don't have to succumb to the high-priced, calorie-laden foods at the airport if you take the time to be so well prepared.

VACATIONS TO STIMULATE YOUR MIND, BODY, AND SOUL

Should you decide to take a two-week vacation, this does not entitle you to become a lounge lizard, lollygaging on a hammock, eating chocolate bon-bons. Of course, with your new commitment to maintaining a healthy lifestyle, you're not going to indulge in this activity, right? Just checking!

QUICK PAINLESS

You can call ahead to the hotel you're staying at and ask if a VCR comes with the room. If not, ask if you can order one. Nine times out of 10, they'll accommodate you.

IF YOU'RE SO INCLINED

Many airlines offer such choices as low-calorie, vegetarian, fruit, low-fat, kosher, diabetic, or Hindu. You have to order no less than 24 hours ahead of time.

Making Your Traveling Time Active Time

Active travel is a booming business nowadays, and why not? Baby-boomers, 77 million strong, have demanded it. You shouldn't have any trouble finding a trip that features the particular activities you enjoy. You can cross-country ski at the New Age Health Spa in New York or enjoy an exhilarating hiking experience at New Life Fitness Vacations in Vermont. They accommodate all fitness levels. The advanced hiker ascends a 4,000-foot mountain, while intermediates and beginners walk along the picturesque Appalachian Trail, and along trails or mountainside streams and a spectacular waterfall.

If you've ever experienced the color of leaves changing in the fall season in the northeast, you'll remember how beautiful it can be.

Serving Up Adventure—Your Way!

Another resource to look into is Far*Away Adventures in Indiana. This company creates luxurious four- to six-day rafting and walking trips that will leave you spiritually and physically recharged, pampered, and relaxed. You'll receive all the benefits of a nature trip combined with the personal attention you'd expect at a private spa. Just think, you'll experience traveling through an otherwise inaccessible nature preserve that's home to mountain lions, black bear, bighorn sheep, deer, golden eagles, and ospreys. Trips take place on the Middle Fork and Main Salmon Rivers, deep in Idaho's River of No Return Wilderness.

The trip starts out with a champagne flight by small plane to the river. The rafting part is up to 40 miles. For first-time rafters, this is for you. The level of fitness is left entirely up to you.

You can also treat yourself to the various services they provide, such as professional massage and body work each night. Gourmet meals are served with crystal and linen on the banks of the river. Yoga, stretch classes, fly-fishing, and inflatable kayaking are offered as well.

If you want to try something similar but want it to include a trip to another country, you can go through the same company, but make your experience happen in Costa Rica, the British Virgin Islands, or the San Juan Islands. I am not promoting this particular company on its own, but using it gives you an awareness of the opportunities that are out there. Global Fitness Adventures offers similar opportunities that include windsurfing, scuba diving, horseback riding, snow-shoeing, trout-fishing, downhill skiing, and even Indian drumming and dance workshops! Wow! And you thought your "golden years" should be about a laid back, wait until you go to your great reward experience! All of this is just to show you that the best things are yet to come!

Going by Sea

Does the idea of a Sea Spa sound intriguing? Well, this is what you can expect from some companies: Windstar Cruises offer a yacht! If you want to know the precise location, you may just have to ask the captain. If it's summer, you'll embark on this lovely yacht in Nice, France. If it's winter, expect to leave from Barbados and sail the Caribbean.

IF YOU'RE SO
INCLINED

Taking a vacation in New England during leaf changing season is also a great opportunity for you creative types to bring your camera, paint brushes, and easel.

You'll be able to sail and stop by various villages, shop, enjoy the pristine beaches, or go on an excursion to the inland rain forests or ancient ruins. On board your every need will be catered to, and you can be active day and night, or do nothing but meditate, read, and relax.

Some of the activities included are fitness programs, hydrotherapy, stress management, skin care, steam and sauna rooms, and swimming in the aqua-fit pool. Instruction is also available in waterskiing, windsurfing, snorkeling, and sailing.

A plethora of opportunities you say? Well, hold on to your Stairmaster, there are even spas specializing in weight loss.

BUT WHERE CAN I FIND OUT MORE?

To find out more, call the International Spa & Resort Association, a clearing house for spa resort information. In addition, you could call Spa Finders. Prices for a four-day stay range from $350 to $4,000.

Cruise ships offer state-of-the-art gyms, walking programs and a swimming pool. Your recreationally challenged loved one can participate in shuffleboard, Ping-Pong, or bingo while you take the aerobics class.

For those really adventurous souls, you can get involved in ice climbing in the Canadian Rockies, dog-sledding across the Alaskan tundra, cave exploring, para-sailing, or just about anything you can think of. Check out some of the adventure travel companies such as Mountain Travel-Sobeki and Overseas Adventure Travel.

YOU'LL THANK YOURSELF LATER

For those couples or families who may be in conflict with the new you, you should seriously consider something like Club Med or a cruise ship.

Getting Time on Your Side

	The Old Way	The Lazy Way
Selecting a gym away from home	2 hours	1 minute
Pointless socializing	3 hours	5 minutes
Finding a trip that works for everyone	Impossible!	20 minutes
Enjoying your vacations	There's a 50 percent chance on that one!	Every time!
Being afraid to try something a little new	All the time	Not anymore! (I got all my questions answered first!)
Planning to take a fantasy vacation	Years	10 minutes

twelve

Overnight Success

My mother—a published author of 27 novels and a real "'90s woman"—was my role model. She was way ahead of her time when it came to independence and true grit. I later found out that she was quite the tomboy and loved the outdoors. She traveled with her colleagues who were also mystery writers and took advantage of every chance to get the most out of life.

THE BEGINNING OF THE STORY

Her father, who fought in the Boer War and who was later relegated to working in the diamond mines in South Africa as a prisoner, left her an unusual legacy. It seems that when he contracted rheumatic fever from the dampness of the mines, he developed heart trouble.

He later learned English from the soldiers guarding him and used his fluency to help him escape and wend his way to America. It turns out that he met my grandmother on the ship that was transporting him to America and later married her, even though he knew that because of his heart trouble, he was going to die at an early age. His philosophy was to live

If your beliefs don't quite jive with the God concept, perhaps you could set your mind on another higher influence that you do recognize and let that influence be the focal point of your "process" toward spiritual growth.

each day as if it were his last. He died of a heart attack at age 42.

My mom practiced this principle in all of her affairs and passed it down to me, now I'm passing it on to you.

Seeing the Point

You can imagine how shocked I was a few years ago when I first learned that my mother was in a downward decline mentally and physically. She started getting lost when she would go out for an errand, and her checkbook mistakes were quite obvious and frequent. She started questioning the motives of her closest friends and even got in a fistfight with a neighbor, because my mom accused her of stealing her rake. This was so unlike the woman I had learned so much from. I was later informed that she was in the grips of the beginning stage of Alzheimer's disease.

As you can expect, I was shattered. Suddenly the one who had become my emotional foundation and greatest cheerleader for my life was becoming a child! This was hard for me to accept. It is much easier to take care of a small child, who grows up and learns to take responsibility and subsequently goes on to take care of herself. But the rock of Gibraltar—my mom—suddenly needed a baby-sitter? I had to watch as she reverted back to being a child and eventually an infant. I could not believe this. Suddenly my foundation was rocked! What should I do? Who could I talk to? How was I to continue with my career, support myself financially, and attend to this critical situation?

Does this sound all too familiar? Well, read on, because no matter what you're going through, you can handle this and any other situation that "comes with the territory" as you advance in age. This includes situations like suddenly having to let your adult children come back to live with you and maybe even caring for your grandchildren due to the inability of your own grown children to handle this responsibility. You may even have to attend to your spouse or lover, who could be suffering from myriad situations.

ACCEPTING AND LETTING GO

The first step in reference to any situation you may face is acceptance. Acceptance is the key to maintaining your peace of mind no matter what life sends your way.

TEACH YOURSELF THROUGH IT

The next thing to do is to seek information about the particular problem you're facing. This will help eliminate the anxiety and frustration you'll be feeling. By clarifying your challenges ahead, you'll be better equipped to deal with your situation.

I've made out a list of other things you can do to take control of your situation, instead of letting it take control of you.

- Seek information. Family support meetings can put you in touch with vital resources.

- Take action. Seek out a professional who specializes in the problem for advice.

YOU'LL THANK YOURSELF LATER

Learn the serenity prayer and use it: "God grant me the serenity to accept the things I cannot change, the courage to change the things I can, and the wisdom to know the difference."

- Weigh findings. Get second opinions and get a family decision about what needs to be done.

- Identify resources. Availability of transportation, family, and friends to assist in the caregiver's role.

- Plan care. Your life will be changed by this situation, so you need to plan accordingly.

DEALING WITH THE STRESS

Let's face it, the physical, mental, and spiritual condition of the patient determines the amount of stress you'll exhibit. Your well-being is essential to your being able to handle this new intrusion on your life. But read on, there is definitely hope. I got through it, and I'm going to lead you through it.

The important thing is not to put too many expectations on yourself. Anger, guilt, frustration, and similar feelings may push you to your limits. Believe me, you'll thank yourself later if you can keep from adding to your burdens.

ONE IS THE LONELIEST NUMBER— HELP YOURSELF!

Finally, the process of getting help will encourage you to become a unique individual again as you reconstruct your own life and prepare for the future. You'll also experience a broad array of physical, mental, and behavioral changes.

If you're unfamiliar with these stresses and strains, you may begin to think that you're losing your mind. As you experience the loss of your loved one, you may even

YOU'LL THANK YOURSELF LATER

For a caregiver who experiences frequent financial problems, family meetings to discuss possibilities and an investigation of community resources may prove helpful. Feeling isolated and abandoned is common, so other people showing their care and concern can help.

feel you're losing yourself as well. This is the true essence of grief, but remember that it's through grief that we come into the process of healing. In order to heal, you must go through the "process." It's imperative that you do not try to resist this phase. This is a crucial time for individual growth and development.

As the illness of your loved one progresses, your stress level increases, and if you're not careful, you could develop stress-related health problems. But relax, by following my simple guidelines, you won't have to be so uncomfortable as you face the inevitable changes one faces as they march to and through their "golden years." Realize that you're just facing life's daily challenges and changes, which you can master and grow from. You can rise above life's challenges and through it all, create a more fulfilling life—the life you want to live. My concepts and suggestions will give you a road map for a spiritual journey as well, and a life that is richly blessed.

WILLING YOURSELF THROUGH IT

We all have the gift of free will, given to us by our creator. Free will allows us to make individual decisions based on God's divine will for our lives, but it also lets us choose to go off in another direction if we want to—our will. That is why divine and unconditional love can be found to fill a void in our lives.

I believe that our brief presence on earth is to help us develop maximum spiritual strength. We prosper in this direction when we're aligned with God's will. To feel the touch of God's love, we need to exhibit our own loving

YOU'LL THANK YOURSELF LATER

To heal, you must accept the reality of death and the reality of it as you work through the pain. The idea for healing here is to accept life on life's terms. This is done through accepting the fact that the loved one is no longer on your planet. You must emotionally transfer them as you move on with your life and prepare yourself to move forward with your life.

Although I tend to speak in terms of the Christian form of the divine, your faith is your strength, whether your worship involves a male figure, female figure, or the simplicity of nature itself. I can't say it often enough, this is part of your strength, no matter what form it takes!

kindness and live totally in divine love. From here we can ascend to an experience of perfect peace and harmony in our lives. For every decision made that is based solely on the self, we dim our perception of God and open ourselves up to very unpleasant experiences designed to show us where we were wrong.

I am not asking you to depart from your personal convictions. I am simply stating that through the knowledge of God's divine love, His help and guidance are offered to all, regardless of your religious preferences.

LOVING THROUGH LIFE

Recognizing our spiritual destiny does not depend on professing allegiance to a particular source of religious worship. The key is to live a life full of love. The daily choices based on the precepts discussed here are key to your quality of life. This is the path required for your mental, physical, and spiritual well-being.

Taking Positive Action

Wouldn't it be great if we had a magic wand to wave any time we wanted to shift from fear to hope, from anger to laughter, from loneliness to a room full of love? The positive moments give us undeniable joy and are immensely fulfilling. Aren't these feelings a direct outgrowth of prolonged thoughts and feelings prodded by specific situations? These feelings slowly invade the externals of our lives. If we are optimistic, our relationships have a tendency to grow. It can help us take a chance to pursue our dreams and to reach our goals.

Constructive thoughts, beliefs, and attitudes can create the life we want, while destructive ones can block our attempts. Wishful thinking does not work here; action is a requisite.

The by-product of free will is freedom, and with that comes a great responsibility. With each choice we make, we create something. When we choose to react to people, places, and things, we set up a pattern of habit. If you constantly react in anger, you'll become habitually argumentative and angry. That's why it's hard to make instantaneous changes in our thoughts and actions. The hope is not to blind ourselves to our undesirable habits. We can transform and change by acting our way into right thinking. We can use our great power of will to build constructive routes away from negative thoughts, attitudes, and beliefs.

JOURNALING

Another way to create your spiritual growth is through **journaling.** This involves keeping a daily account of your experiences as you perform some of the exercises offered here. You should not only note the external events in your life, but also spend time putting to paper the kind of inner activity you experienced. Record your emotional reactions as well. A good book to get with regards to a format for this is by Dr. Mark Thurston in the A.R.E. home-study course called "How to Change Your Attitudes and Emotions."

IF YOU'RE SO
INCLINED

You might try some of these spiritual affirmations:

- "Thank you Father for being with me as I face this trial."

- "God is with me in this trial and all trials. He does not will that I perish."

- "The joy of love is in the loving."

THE POWER OF PRAYER

Our ability to pray is the most precious of all our human endeavors. This enables us to communicate with our Creator and feel close to Him. By doing so, we open ourselves to the unlimited aid He offers us. Through prayer we're able to unlock the healing power of our inner spirit by depending on the outer presence of our Higher Power.

After we pray, we enter meditation to hear God's answer. In the silence of meditation, we open ourselves to God and allow the healing power of His spirit to transform us mentally, physically, and spiritually. Following are suggestions on contents to be covered in prayer:

- Ask our interpretation of the divine to bless others and
- To ask forgiveness of our deeds
- To offer our service for others to the divine
- To turn our lives and will over to the care of the divine
- Ask that divine will be done and for the power to carry that out

You may try some of these other techniques as well:

- Select a favorite standard prayer
- Make up your own prayer
- Pray sincerely, from the depth of your soul

CREATING A PERSONAL POWER

Affirmations and visualization are two techniques, creating a power within your mind to build a specific awareness we consider desirable. We are actually helping to manifest something we want to be true on a physical plane. Affirmations are similar to prayers. Prayers are to God, and affirmations are for ourselves to hear and internalize.

Visualization may just involve a single mental picture. It can also unfold a complicated scenario with complex locales, people, and activities. Visualization can include imaginings of impressions through auditory, olfactory, and sensory perceptions.

TAKING STOCK

The next exercise to help catapult you into Nirvana includes a self-inventory. This activity allows you to sort out the confusion and contradiction present in your life. By doing this, you find out who you really are and proceed to start on the path to positive change. This will help you get rid of the burdens and traps that are preventing you from growth, and it will provide you with the turning point you need in your life. You'll free yourself of old, useless patterns.

To Thine Own Self Be True

It's time to take stock, to honestly evaluate yourself and your life up to this moment in time. Take a few moments to consider the following questions:

YOU'LL THANK YOURSELF LATER

It is wise to choose in advance a positive affirmation or visualization so your mind will be focused and you don't drift off into a negative energy field.

Pick a time of day where you can do your self-evaluation. How about making an appointment with yourself after your prayer and meditation? At this time, you'll be more open to inner guidance.

- Spiritually and mentally, where are you and where do you want to be?

- What are the steps you need to take to get there?

- What do you feel you need to change about your past?

- Allow yourself to face your resentments, frustrations, guilt, shame, fear, denial, and anxiety. By doing this, you'll begin the process of overcoming these things.

- Celebrate your assets: honesty, caring, kindness, and generosity. It's too easy to contemplate our negative points, but now is the time to honestly consider the good we bring to ourselves and others.

You also need to include any pertinent information on relationships. Where are you at fault? Are you willing to admit it? Write it down. By reviewing your past history mentally, physically, and spiritually, and looking at where you are now, you're in a position to uncover, discover, and discard: the 3 Ds! You're putting yourself in a position to embark on a journey to self-development and true happiness that you can give to yourself and that no one can take away.

So you've sat and thought about all of this stuff, but now what?

- Write your answers in your journal.

- Reread your journal after a few days to help gain a new perspective.

Throughout all of this, you're developing positive actions, affirmations, prayer, and visualization, and creating a purposeful way to look at the world and perhaps to make the best of a bad situation. You'll restore hope from within when life throws you those little curve balls that could cause you to become discouraged.

You'll be able to discover joy in difficult situations. Regardless of your circumstances, you have the power to decide what thoughts, attitudes, and feelings you allow into your mind. You'll even develop a sense of humor about life as you go along. You reap the ultimate reward when you take the appropriate action to your worrisome circumstances and experience a spiritual awakening by doing so.

THE POWER OF BELIEF

Do you have a dream or an area that you want to conquer in your life? Go after it with faith and mentally picture yourself achieving it. Know that belief gets results. The answer is to believe: in the divine, in yourself, and in your future. Believe that you can and believe in people. Believe and just keep on believing.

YOU'LL THANK YOURSELF LATER

Replace worry with faith. Develop determined, optimistic attitudes with positive affirmations.

Getting Time on Your Side

	The Old Way	The Lazy Way
Putting on a happy face	4 hours	5 minutes
Finding someone to love	Years	5 minutes
Realizing your dreams	Never	I take another step every day
Keeping positive	Impossible	A few minutes
Being able to believe in yourself and others	Never	Every day
Accomplishing miracles	Years	10 minutes

More Lazy Stuff

How to Get Someone Else to Do It

No matter how much you've read about techniques used to retard the aging process, covering the gamut of topics as I've presented here, a little help from a professional can go a long way to sending you down the right road to age-defying success. If you ignore these suggestions, you may just be throwing good money after bad and wasting time, which is not the purpose of this book. The following is a list of areas to consider for outside and professional help:

- Exercise prescriptions
- Plastic surgery
- Weight loss
- Alternative medicine
- Nutritional supplements
- Resorts
- Spas
- Stress reduction
- Elder care

YOU'D BETTER SHOP AROUND!

Don't call the first professional person or company you run across. Compile a list based on third-party referrals. Start out by checking the Yellow Pages for the services you're looking for.

Keep your eyes open at beauty salons, health food stores, magazines, local daily newspapers, and gyms for seminars focusing on your area of interest.

Arrange an interview. You need to talk to the professional even if you decide to use them just once. It is important you have the right "chemistry." You won't benefit by working with someone who gets on your nerves.

Here are some things to keep in mind:

- Check credentials. Is your professional licensed?
- Is he/she educated in his/her field?
- Does he/she keep up on the latest research? How long has he/she been in business?
- What is his/her client base? You want someone with a solid background, somebody who understands his/her particular area of expertise.

Get all quotes for services up front. Ask to see client contracts, and have the service provide you with a sample contract between you and them. Get the exact description of service they will be providing for you.

You'll love the time and energy you save when facing the time constraints you have in the first place! Remember, above all, you want to do it *The Lazy Way*!

If You Really Want More, Read These

ON THE SHELVES

If you suddenly develop an interest in any areas I've covered here, I've recommended some book titles you can find at your local bookstore.

Balch, James F., M.D. and Phyllis A. Balch, C.N.C. *Prescription for Nutritional Healing: A Practical A-Z Reference to Drug-Free Remedies using Vitamins, Minerals, Herbs, and Food Substances,* Avery Pub Group, 1996

Clare, Sally and David Clare, *Creative Vegetarian Cookery,* Prism Press, 1988

Hill, Napoleon, *The Law of Success,* Success Unlimited, 1969

Hoffman, S.B. & Platt, C.A., *Comforting the Confused,* Springer Publishing, 1991

Lakin, M., *When Someone You Love Has Alzheimer's Disease,* Dell Publishing, 1995

Lark, Susan, *Anxiety and Stress Self Help Book: Effective Solutions for Nervous Tension, Emotional Distress, Anxiety, and Panic,* Celestial Arts, 1996

Mindell, Earl, Ph.D., *Vitamin Bible,* Mass Market Paberback, 1991

—— *Secret Remedies: The Essential Guide To Treating Common Ailments with Vitamins, Minerals, Herbs, and Other Cutting Edge Remedies,* Fireside, 1998

—— *Prescription Alternatives,* Keats Pub, 1998

Paavo, Airola, *How to Keep Slim, Healthy, and Young with Juice Fasting,* Health Plus Publishers, 1972

Salomon, Maureen, *All Your Health Questions Answered Naturally,* Bay to Bay Distribution, Inc., 1998

Smith, Robert C., *Attitude and Your Life,* ARE Press, 1998

Weider, Joe and Betty Weider, *The Weider Book of Bodybuilding Tips and Routines,* Contemporary Books, 1982

ON THE NET

For you computer and Internet geeks, you can look up many things under the health and lifestyle Internet chats. Also for anti-aging info, go to my Web page, www.jmyers/foutnofyuth.html. I have links! (And I don't mean golf!)

If you're hunting for the perfect place to sun and have fun, or just to get yourself a culture shock, key into the Internet Travel Network (www.itn.net). Fare mail is cool! Need a flight tomorrow? Register at Expedia (www.expedia.com).

If You Don't Know What It Means, Look Here

I'm not saying you're dunce material by including this section, it's just a refresher course in case you forgot the difference between a bar, weight, or machine.

Antioxidant: A substance that blocks the destructive oxidation reactions of the body. Examples include vitamins C and E, the minerals selenium and germanium, the enzymes catalase and superoxide dismutase (SOD), coenzyme Q10, and some amino acids.

Biofeedback: This is a technique for helping an individual become conscious of usually unconscious body processes, such as heartbeat or body temperature, so that he or she can gain some measure of control over them, and thereby learn to manage the effects of various disorders.

Cholesterol: A crystalline substance that is soluble in fats and produced by all vertebrates. It's a necessary constituent of cell membranes, and facilitates the transport and absorption of fatty acids. Excess cholesterol is bad for your health.

Dementia: Acquired impairment of intellectual function that results in a marked decline of memory, language ability, personality, visuo-spatial skills, and or cognition (orientation, perception reasoning, abstract thinking, and calculation).

Homeopathy: Use of a variety of plants, animal, or mineral substances in very small doses to stimulate the body's natural healing powers and to bring the body back into balance.

Hormone: Substance produced by the endocrine gland that regulates a bodily function.

Hypertension: High blood pressure. Defined as anything over a resting pressure 140/90 reading.

Laser: An instrument that focuses highly amplified light rays. Can be used in surgery, including surgery of the eye. Also used for improvement of skin.

Menopause: The cessation of menstruation, caused by a sharp decrease in the production of the sex hormones estrogen and progesterone. Follows after the age of 45 or the removal of the female reproductive system.

Naturopathy: The use of herbs, diet, and other natural methods and substances to cure illness. This technique is used to stimulate the body's immune system without the use of various medicines.

Osteoporosis: Occurs when minerals leak out of bones, rendering them more porous and fragile.

Seratonin: A neurotransmitter found in the brain, considered essential for relaxation and concentration.

It's Time for Your Reward

Once You've Done This...	Reward Yourself!...
Blasted some fat with housercize	Watch your favorite sitcom!
Booked an adventure travel package	Buy a new music CD
Enjoyed a successful meditation	Enjoy a bubble bath!
Rid your home of unhealthy food	Treat yourself to a gourmet meal!
Managed your time effectively for one week	Go see a movie matinee!
Set up your meditative spot complete with a mat, dim lighting, incense, and a mini-stereo system for your favorite music	Buy yourself a meditation tape
Visited a plastic surgeon for an "appraisal"	Treat yourself to some low-fat frozen yogurt
Assembled your anti-aging beauty kit	Get a manicure!
Learned to believe in yourself	Sleep in!
Found a workout buddy for regular exercise dates	Take an afternoon and go shopping together!

Index

Stop Aging
The Lazy Way

Now is the best time to make the changes you want! Time to get into the best shape of your life, to extend your youthful years, and enjoy life to the fullest. Just spread your wings to be the best you can be.

This is what you can achieve when you put it all together!

Seeing the results from your hard work, whether it is a taut stomach or finishing your "housercize" program in minutes, is an accomplishment. An accomplishment is sometimes just doing one of your "Lazy Way" tasks. You don't have to set any personal records here! Just completing something is your own reward. Why? Because it feels so good! No matter who you are, no matter what you have gone through, you can do this program in only a few minutes a day.

I am living proof that it's never too late to break out of a rut.

If you need extra motivation, just log on to my www.fountainyouth.com! Good luck!! I have done it, the thousands of people I have worked with have done it, and so can you! Before long, you'll be brimming with optimism because you know that no matter how good the past has been, the future is going to be even better.

Middle Age is "the bomb!"

With a new-found self-confidence, you will constantly take on bigger challenges—no longer hiding out in the comfort zone. You will know that whatever happens in your life—no matter how rapidly the changes occur—you will be able to evolve and constantly improve. So I ask you, which will it be? Confidence...or temerity? Seems like a simple decision, but in reality, it is an opportunity of a lifetime! Fulfill your potential—you can do it.

Don't just think about it...Do It!

Now you can do these tasks, too!

The Lazy Way

Starting to think there are a few more of life's little tasks that you've been putting off? Don't worry—we've got you covered. Take a look at all of *The Lazy Way* books available. Just imagine—you can do almost anything *The Lazy Way!*

Handle Your Money The Lazy Way
By Sarah Young Fisher and Carol Turkington
0-02-862632-X

Build Your Financial Future The Lazy Way
By Terry Meany
0-02-862648-6

Cut Your Spending The Lazy Way
By Leslie Haggin
0-02-863002-5

Have Fun with Your Kids The Lazy Way
By Marilee Lebon
0-02-863166-8

Keep Your Kids Busy The Lazy Way
By Barbara Nielsen and Patrick Wallace
0-02-863013-0

Feed Your Kids Right The Lazy Way
By Virginia Van Vynckt
0-02-863001-7

*All Lazy Way books are just $12.95!

additional titles on the back!